THE OAKWOOD PRESS

# A Pictorial Guide
# ALPINE RAILWAYS

*Mervyn Jones*

© Oakwood Press & Mervyn Jones 2009
British Library Cataloguing in Publication Data
A Record for this book is available from the British Library
ISBN 978 0 85361 690 0
Typeset by Oakwood Graphics.
Repro by PKmediaworks, Cranborne, Dorset.
Printed by Cambrian Printers, Aberystwyth, Ceredigion.

# Biographical Note

Mervyn Jones has had a lifetime interest in railways since the early 1950s when the 'LMS' was his passion. After retiring from a long career in public service in 1997, he has spent much of his time with his wife in Europe, spending some of their time studying railways in a number of countries.

Whilst he has previously published extensively academic texts, in 2006 he wrote and illustrated his first railway book, *The Essential Guide to French Heritage and Tourist Railways*. In 2007, he followed this with *The Essential Guide to Swiss Heritage and Tourist Railways* and then, in 2008, he produced *The Essential Guide to Austrian Railways and Tramways*; all published by The Oakwood Press. He is currently researching and photographing for *The Essential Guide to Welsh Heritage and Scenic Railways*.

He lives with his wife, Caroline, half the year at their home on the North Wales, Shropshire and Cheshire border and the other half in the south of France between Avignon and Nîmes.

*Front cover:* The Dolomites as seen from between Welsberg and Niederdorf with a Stadler-built FLIRT No. ETR.155.003 travelling towards Brunico on 9th March, 2009.  *Author*

*Title page:* ÖBB railcar No. 4024 069-9 on the Giselabahn in Austria heading for Kitzbühel from St Johann in Tirol on 10th March, 2009.  *Author*

*Rear cover:* Train de Pignes - Five-Lille No. 326 *Bretonne* crossing Pont-de-la-Reine-Jeanne near Annot on 14th May, 2006.  *Author*

Published by The Oakwood Press (Usk), P.O. Box 13, Usk, Mon., NP15 1YS.
E-mail:   sales@oakwoodpress.co.uk
Website:  www.oakwoodpress.co.uk

# Contents

Rhätische Bahn locomotive No. 52 *Brusio* heads the Bernina Express on the Montebello curve towards Tirano on 6th October, 2006. *Caroline Jones*

# Introduction

Where is the loudest sounding church bell in the world? Where did the meringue originate? Where is a Passion Play performed once every 10 years? Where is the largest glacier in Europe? Which is largest inland lake in Europe? Where did Hitler and Mussolini meet to celebrate the 'Pact of Steel'? Which company first produced the spinning reel for game fishing? Which was the first town in the world to install electric street lighting? Who were called the 'Salt Princes'? Where did Sherlock Holmes meet his end? Where in Europe are brown bears still living in the wild? Where is there a life-sized statue of Freddie Mercury?

The answers to these questions and many more can be found in this publication. General knowledge is an unlikely subject to feature in a book about railways. However, this is a different type of book. In researching and writing about alpine railways, the author, in addition to information about the prime subject matter, has chosen to include what he hopes are interesting facts about the places through which trains pass.

This book is the first *Pictorial Guide* on European Railways to be produced by the author. It follows on the successes of *Essential Guide* series on European Railways centred on the French (2006), Swiss (2007) and Austrian (2008) guides published by The Oakwood Press. However, this book is radically different from the previous publications in a number of ways.

There is a far greater concentration on the pictorial representation of the railways/routes with an emphasis on the picturesque nature of the Alpine railway scene. Incidentally, all the photographs are new and have not featured in any of the previous three publications although the sharp-eyed reader may identify one or two photographs of a similar origin.

The focus on presenting photographs has led to a change in the book's format, i.e. from a portrait to a landscape layout. This has allowed the pictures to occupy a full-size page. Hopefully, the reader will be able to enjoy a greater and more detailed appreciation of alpine railway scenes. However, moving from a portrait layout and at same time maintaining the approximate size (and cost!) of the earlier books does not come without sacrifice.

Given that the previous guides were heavy on detailed information about rolling stock, railway history, operating dates, tariffs and so on, most of this does not feature in this book in order to give sufficient room for the photographs. It is also means that those who read this book will not be subjected to a replication of the previous French, Swiss and Austrian guides. On the contrary, those earlier books complement this one by meeting the enthusiast's desire for more information about the railways listed. Unfortunately, however, Essential Guides have not yet been written on German, Italian or Slovenian/Croatian railways. This will necessitate, therefore, the inquisitive reader to pursue his or her researches elsewhere. For more about this, see the 'Getting the best out of this Guide' section later.

Research for this book began in 2004, although at that time it was aimed at gathering material and photographs to produce what later turned out to be the Essential French guide. Studies expanded over the following four years eventually leading to the publication of the Swiss, and later, Austrian Essential guides. From the beginning of 2008, the focus became gathering material in Italy, Slovenia/Croatia and Germany, along with re-visits to the earlier countries to 'sweep up' missing material, mainly photographs, as well update previous information.

In sum, 14 separate location tours have been made over those years accounting for over 160 days on site. In excess of 6,500 digital photographs have been taken using a variety of Nikon DSLR cameras and lenses. Having built such a large photographic library there has been no need, in producing this publication, to repeat photographs which have appeared in previous Essential Guides. Every attempt has been made to ensure that the information produced is up-to-date. However, like most things in life, the world is constantly changing, a phenomenon applying equally to railways as to anything else. The reader is asked, therefore, to treat the content as a 'snapshot' of what the situation was in 2008/9.

It also has to be said that the book has attempted to identify most of the railways running in or to and from the Alps. The choice made by the author was to take a relief map of the Alps and consider those railways that operate in the area of a mountain or mountains. Various definitions abound as to what can be defined as a 'mountain'. For the purposes of this book the author, who is by no means an orologist, has chosen, rightly or wrongly, to identify in this book those landforms which reach peaks of, or in excess of 610

m (2,000 feet) above sea level. The railways listed here are by no means exhaustive, but the author hopes that very few are absent.

This *Pictorial Guide to Alpine Railways* identifies a total of 142 railways or routes which can be found in the alpine areas of any one of seven European countries. Listed are 20 in France, 29 in Italy, six in Slovenia, one in Croatia, 34 in Austria, 19 in Germany and 33 in Switzerland. Each railway has been given a unique entry and all but two have been photographed. The total number of photographs amounts to 143 and, except for three, have been taken by the author or his wife. It is sincerely hoped that the pictures give as much pleasure to the reader as they did to the photographers who took them. Enjoy!

# Acknowledgements

The author acknowledges the help, support, advice and, indeed, friendship, he has received from many, both in the UK and abroad, during the research, photography and later writing of this guide.

It is not practical to identify all those who helped by name but, nonetheless, their individual contributions are very much appreciated. Throughout the research, in France, Italy, Slovenia, Croatia, Austria, Germany and Switzerland and, later, in the United Kingdom, the author has been impressed with the enthusiastic support he has been given. Mention must also be given to many members of the enthusiasts' associations in the UK interested in European railways, viz. the SNCF Society, Italian Railways Society, Austrian Railway Group, German Railways Society and Swiss Railways Society; their help and advice has been much appreciated. In France the FACS-UNECTO organisation has always been most helpful.

As with the earlier publications, the author thanks The Oakwood Press, and, in particular, their Ian Kennedy, for his patience, his encouragement, his useful comments and the most helpful suggestions he provided.

Finally, the author gives special thanks to his wife, Caroline. Not only did she take many of the photographs included in this book, but also she uncomplainingly supported him throughout the project. She accompanied him on all the numerous site visits often patiently waiting for yet another train to pass. During the writing up of the guide, she gave much needed encouragement and advice as well as helpful, critical appraisal of the text.

Notwithstanding the valued support given from all quarters, the responsibility for all errors and omissions rests with the author.

# Getting the best out of this Guide

To assist the reader in navigating his, or her, way to the railways/routes identified in this guide they have been organized as follows. The seven countries, which enjoy alpine railways, are listed in the order of an imaginary journey. Beginning in the southeast of **France**, the traveller crosses the border into **Italy** and runs across the northern part of the country to Trieste and Udine before entering **Slovenia**. The tour there centres on the west and north of Ljubljana with a very short detour into **Croatia**. Heading north the traveller enters **Austria** visiting mainly the centre and west of that country before moving north again into **Germany**, or more precisely, Bavaria. The traveller then continues east and eventually into **Switzerland** passing through the central and southern cantons to reach the end of the journey.

Each country's railway/route is awarded a unique alpha/numeric reference using the international road users' identification code as the basis, viz. France (F), Italy (I), Slovenia (SLO), Croatia (HR), Austria (A), Germany (D) and Switzerland (CH). It will not be surprising to find that many of the railways are international in nature and, therefore, can be identified in more than one country. Where this is the case, and in order to avoid duplication of information, cross-referencing is used extensively. Some cross border routes, however, do have entries in more than one country, the Centovalli railway between Italy and Switzerland being a good example. In so doing, and to avoid repetition, the author has attempted to provide separate information in each entry, the full description of the whole gained by taking advantage of the cross reference.

Unlike the previous guides, the content has been written in such a way as to appeal (hopefully) to a wider audience than just the die-hard railway enthusiast. This book, therefore, may frustrate the latter, although it is hoped that the pictorial aspects will satisfy many. To assist those who would wish to gain more information, here are a number of suggestions. Firstly, those who have not read the previous *Essential Guides* for France, Switzerland and Austria

may find help there. Secondly, there are many other publications which can help and the best of these are listed in the *Bibliography*. Thirdly, the Internet increasingly is a quickly accessed source of comprehensive information; to help in this respect useful websites are listed in the text. A list has also been included with websites the author has found useful together with a list of related organizations and their addresses.

Many of the publications and websites are not always written in English. Again, to help, some foreign words are explained in parentheses. There is also Glossary of some common railway terms in five languages with English translations. The Glossary also includes certain abbreviations expanded.

Every attempt has been made to ensure that all the information in this guide is correct and up-to-date, but it is important to render a health warning. Before travelling any distance to any of the locations listed herein, it is wise, in order to avoid disappointment, to check the state of current operations. There are many factors in heritage and tourist railway operations, short of closure or suspension, which can alter the availability of a service, not least of all the changing condition of many of the ageing locomotives and other rolling stock. In addition, much preserved railway material can and does move around its country of residence and sometimes, the continent. The advice is, therefore, if the reader wishes to see something in particular, it is wise to check the whereabouts beforehand.

Another issue of particular importance is, having seen something of interest in this book, how does the would-be visitor find it? In each of the 142 separate entries, the main towns through which the railways travel are provided; these should help the reader, using other sources, to identify the exact locations. In writing this book, the author gave much thought as to whether to provide maps for each of the entries or collections of them. The priority of this publication, from the outset, has been to provide a pictorial essay about the Alps and its Railways with some supporting text. The limitations of space therefore, and the fact that the author is not a cartographer, combine to exclude what many might otherwise criticize as inadequate maps were they to be provided. In sum, therefore, there are no maps. The author is aware, however, of the excellent publications whose priorities are the provision of comprehensive and detailed railway mapping. In particular, Switzerland, Austria and Germany are individually addressed by the excellent Schweers + Wall publications, the European Railway Atlases produced by M.G. Ball (covering Italy, France and others) and the helpful Thomas Cook's Rail Map – Europe. These are all commended by the author (*see Bibliography*).

Given the mountainous nature of the Alps some railways need a system which allows trains that cannot rely on normal adhesion alone to negotiate steep gradients. This need led to the invention of the various rack/cogwheel systems which have played a crucial part in bringing railways to otherwise inaccessible locations. Rack/cogwheel systems are given frequent mention throughout this book and are described in more detail in the *Appendix*.

An Index is also provided. Listed by country are all the railways featured in this book together with their Michelin map references and page numbers.

Every attempt has been made to provide as much information as is possible in a book of this size and type. However, it is inevitable, given the enormity of the subject addressed, that it has only been possible to scratch the surface. This book is no encyclopaedia. Hopefully, though, what the reader sees and reads here may whet the appetite to explore further. In other words, this book is only the start of the railway journey through the Alps and not its conclusion.

Safe journey! *Bon voyage! Buon viaggio! Srecno pot! Sretan put! Gute Reise!*

# The Alps Defined

The Alps is the principal collection of mountain ranges in Europe extending nearly 260,000 square kilometres and embraces parts of seven main countries, i.e. France, Italy, Slovenia, Austria, Germany, Switzerland and Liechtenstein. The mountains run in parallel from a south-westerly to a north-easterly direction for well over a distance of one thousand kilometres beginning near to tFrance's Mediterranean coast at Colle d'Altare and concluding at the Hochschwab on the eastern side of Austria.

The highest mountain in the range is Mont Blanc in France reaching a height of 4,807 metres (15,774 ft). Other mountains include such notables as the Matterhorn, the Eiger, Monte Rosa, Zugsptize, and the Gross Glockner. The permanent snow line is upwards from about 3,000 metres above sea level. It is reported by the Union Internationale des Associations d'Alpinisme (UIAA) that there are 82 mountains in the Alps with summits of or over 4,000 metres (13,123 ft). Karl Blodig, an Austrian optician, at the age of 52 years was the first man to have climbed all the peaks over 4,000 metres. The Alpine air must have been good for him for he did not die until within a month of his 97th birthday.

The Alpine ranges provide sources for many important European rivers, i.e. the Rhine, Po, Tagliamento, Piave, Adige and the Rhône. These great rivers variously feed the North Sea, the Mediterranean, the Adriatic and the Black Sea.

The Alps came about as a result of the catastrophic meeting of Africa's and Europe's tectonic plates which, with the following rains, snows and frosts, caused rivers and glaciers to be formed which sculptured the mountains into their present form.

The Alpine economy features agricultural, service and manufacturing industries, examples of the latter being the production of textiles, clocks, watches, chocolate and wooden goods. Since the 19th century mountaineering and skiing interests have come to prominence and which are met by highly-developed tourist facilities including extensive hotel accommodation and transportation systems.

The Alps overall can be defined according to a number of ranges. (NB: The highest summits in each of the ranges are recorded in brackets.)

The **Western Alps** comprises the Alpes-Maritimes (Cima Sud Argentera 3,297 m), Alpes Cottiennes, known in English as the Cottian Alps, (Monte Viso 3,851 m), Alpes Dauphine (Barre des Ecrins 4,101 m) and the Alpes Graian (Gran Paradiso 4,061 m).

St Bernard dog ready for a rescue on the Matterhorn?            *Author*

The **Middle Alps** comprise Alpi Pennine (Mont Blanc 4,807 m; Monte Rosa 4,634 m; Matterhorn 4,478 m), Alpi Lepontine (Monte Leone 3,552 m), Alpi Retiche known as the Rhaetian Alps (Piz Bernina 4,049 m), Berner Alpen known as the Bernese Alps (Finsteraarhorn 4,274 m; Aletschhorn 4,195 m; Jungfrau 4,158 m), Alpi Orobie (Monte Legnone 2,609 m), Otztaler Alpen (Wildspitze 3,774 m), Dolomiti known as the Dolomites (Marmolada 3,342 m) and the Lechtaler Alpen (Parseierspitze 3,036 m).

The **Eastern Alps** comprise the Zillertaler Alpen or Alpi Aurine (Hochfeiler 3,510 m), Kitzbuhler Alpen (Wilder Kaiser 2,559 m), Karnische Alpen or Carnic Alps (Coglians also known as Hohe Warte 2,780 m), Julijske Alpe or Julian Alps (Triglav 2,864 m), Karawanken Alps (Flochstuhl 2,238 m), the Hohe Tauern or Noric Alps (Gross Glockner 3,797 m) and the Niedere Tauern (Hochgolling 2,863 m).

Finally, there are the Dinarsko gorstvo (or **Dinaric Alps)** a mountain chain in southern Europe beyond Austria, spanning the countries of Slovenia, Croatia, Kosovo, Bosnia and Herzegovina, Serbia, Albania and Montenegro. They have not been included in this book given their geographical separation from the main Alpine range. However, very brief mention is given to those railways close to the Austrian border in Slovenia and Croatia.

Not included in this book are the Jura Mountains, located in France and Switzerland, which it is generally accepted do not qualify as part of the Alps.

The largest cities in the Alps are Grenoble in France (population 157,900) and Innsbruck in Austria (population 117,916). In respect of Alpine Roads and Railways, important passes include the Mont Cenis, the two St Bernard crossings, the Gemmi, the Simplon, St Gotthard, the Splügen, Stilfseijoch (Stelvio), the Plocken and the Brenner. Railway tunnels burrow their way under the Alps at the Col de Fréjus, Lötschberg, Simplon, St Gotthard and the Karawanken.

# France

## Introduction

Our journey through the Alps begins in France where mountain ranges are found in the two French regions of Provençe-Alpes-Côte d'Azur and Rhône-Alpes. French Regions are further sub-divided administratively into *départements* (en. departments) of which there are 96 throughout the country, including two on the island of Corsica. Seven of France's departments are wholly or partly alpine in nature. In Provençe-Alpes-Côte d'Azur, there are four such departments – Var, Hautes-Alpes, Alpes de Haute Provençe and Alpes-Maritimes. In the Rhône-Alpes region, there are three - Haute-Savoie, Savoie and Isère. In addition to the popular winter and summer leisure pursuits, several Alpine mountains are included in the itinerary of the Tour de France cycle race. This annually-organized month-long event presents special challenges to the participants who have to make difficult ascents on passes and mountains such as the Col du Tourmalet (2,115 m), Mont Ventoux (1,912 m), Col du Galibier (2,645 m), Hautacam (1,560 m) and perhaps the most famous, the Alpe d'Huez (1,860 m).

The principal ranges of alpine mountains in France are the Maritime Alps, the Cottian Alps, the Dauphiné Alps, including Belledonne and the Massif des Écrins, the Graian Alps, including Mont Blanc Massif and the Vanoise Massif, and the French Prealps. The highest mountain in the region is Mont Blanc (it. Monte Bianco). 'Mont Blanc' translates as White Mountain and is known in France as the *La Dame Blanche* (en. The White Lady). Mont Blanc, at 4,807 m (15,774 ft) is the highest mountain in all of the Alps and in Europe overall. It is often referred to as the 'Rooftop of Europe'.

The main French city is Grenoble, which is also the largest city in any of the countries that are part of the Alps. Chamonix and Chambéry are also important connurbations. The main road routes out of France into the neighbouring Alps are the Mont Blanc tunnel (11.6 km) from Chamonix to Courmayeur in Italy; the St Bernard Pass from Bourg St Maurice to Courmayeur; Canslebourg to Susa in

Italy through the Col de Mont Cenis; the Fréjus tunnel (13 km) from Modane to Bardonécchia in Italy; Vallorcine to Martigny in Switzerland; Briançon to Oulx in Italy via the Col Montgenèvre; a minor road (D206a) from near St Veran to Casteldelfino in Italy; from Larche to Vinadio in Italy via the Col de Larche; Vinadio can also be reached from Auron via the Col de Lombarda; and, finally, from Breil–sur-Roya to Limone-Piemonte in Italy via the Col de Tende. The Mediterranean coast road, obviously not in the Alps, from Menton to Ventimiglia also gives access into Italy.

The are three prime rail routes out of France into the neighbouring Alpine countries, i.e. from St Gervais-le-Fayet to Martigny in Switzerland via Le Châtelard (on the Mont Blanc Express), from Modane to Oulx (Ligne de Maurienne) and from Nice to Limone-Piemonte (Train des Merveilles). There are a further 17 railway routes operating in the French Alps.

## The Railways

### F1 – Chemin de la Fer de Provence

This railway links Nice in the department of Alpes-Maritimes on France's Côte d'Azur with Dignes-les-Bains in the Hautes-Alpes. Originally constructed in 1891 the train service, since 2007, has been operated by Veolia Transport. The total distance covered by the route is 151 km with the journey taking up to 3½ hours each way. Given the nature of its high terrain (over 1,000 m in places) with its many twists and turns a narrow metre gauge was adopted from the outset. On the way there are 16 bridges and viaducts, 15 metallic bridges and 25 tunnels of which the St Michel is the longest at 3.4 km. On the route there are 15 regular stops and 48 request stops. There are also a further 17 halts popular with hikers seeking out challenging trails to follow. The rail services on this route began life as steam-hauled but are now fulfilled by diesel-

CF de Provence railcar No. 2352 arrives at Puget-Theniers station on 16th September, 2007.                                                                 *Author*

powered railcars with four services operating per day in each direction. Trains leave the station in Nice's rue Alfred Binet and pass northwards through the provençal townships of La Madeleine, Lingostière, Colomars-La-Manda, St Martin-du-Var, and La Tinèe where the route turns west and on to Villars-sur-Var. The next stop is at Touët-sur-Var where the medieval village is pressed dramatically into the cliff face. Moving on, the train then reaches Puget-Theniers. A steam-hauled service operates on this route on Sundays in the summer between Touët-sur-Var, Puget-Theniers and Entrevaux. The first stop after Puget-Theniers is the fortified village of Entrevaux where access to the old town is over an ancient gated bridge. The next large town is Annot and then on to the villages of Le Fugeret, Chaudon-Nortante and Mezel-Chateauredon before reaching the town of Digne-les-Bains and terminus of the line. As its name might suggest, Digne-les-Bains offers thermal bathing facililties which were first developed in Roman times. However, after the Romans departed, the baths fell into disuse and were not re-built until 1982. There are eight hot springs with temperatures reaching 42ºC (107ºF). Digne is also on the famous Route Napoléon, from Nice to Grenoble. It was at Digne, in March 1815, that Napoléon Bonaparte stopped briefly and took lunch on his journey from Elba. More information about times and fares on this most scenic of railways can be obtained from the SNCF-TER website www.trainprovence.com

### F2 – Train de Pignes

Le Train de Pignes (en. Train of the Pine Cones) is operated by the Groupement d'Etudes des Chemin de Fer de Provence (GECP). Originally, the steam service used to operate on Sundays during the summer between Puget-Theniers and the town of Annot further up the line towards Digne-les-Bains. However, that all changed in 2009 when the route was radically altered. In many respects, that is sad for the steam-hauled trains can no longer be seen, as depicted on the rear cover of this book, making their way over the magnificent Pont-de-la-Reine-Jeanne viaduct heading for Annot. Nonetheless, this journey is well-worth taking; indeed, it is a 'must-do' both for rail enthusiasts and holidaymakers alike. Departing at 10.25 the new journey now taken is from Puget-Theniers back down the line towards Nice for just over 10 km before arriving at the picturesque medieval village of Touët-sur-Var where the train stops for 45 minutes. This allows sufficient time for the traveller to explore the interesting upper village perched on the hillside and the lower part running alongside the main road, river and railway. The train then returns up the line stopping briefly at Puget-Theniers before continuing for a further 8 km to the fortified medieval village of Entrevaux. Entrevaux, a most popular tourist location, is magnificent, its site guarding a narrow pass through which the fast-flowing Var flows, or sometimes violently cascades after heavy storms. Like Touët-sur-Var, the village is divided into two sections with the older walled part being accessed over a gated bridge into the narrow dark streets - the ideal place to keep cool in the heat of summer! The modern village lies outside and alongside the main road and the railway. High above the village is a 17th century citadel dominating the area and its surrounding valleys. It is here that the train stops for just over four hours allowing for a typically long French Sunday lunch, taken perhaps in one of the delightful restaurants in the old village. To walk off lunch, take the cobbled route up to the citadel, allowing 20 minutes each way to admire the views, take photographs and replenish oxygen! However, be sure not to miss the train for at 16.30 it makes its final 15 minute journey of the day back to Puget-Theniers. Traction used may be one of three steam locomotives. A diesel locotracteur is also available. For a number of years the mainstay has been *Bretonne*, a 1909-built 230T Fives-Lille No. E327. It is supported by a 1925-built 030T No. 36 *Lulu*. Planned to be returned to steam on the line in 2010 is a 1923-built 120-030T Henschel No. E211 which originally

worked the Train des Pignes between 1988 and 1992. It will be named *Portugaise* to celebrate its original deployments on the Portugese Railways network. The locotracteur was built in 1940 by the Compagnie des Chemin de Fer Departementaux for the Nord d'Indre and Loire rail network. Veolia's regular diesel-powered services to and from Nice and Digne-les-Bains integrate with this heritage railway, thus allowing for a most enjoyable full day out for holiday-makers staying in or close to Nice. The steam service operates on Sundays only between mid-May and mid-October. More information, including times and fares, about this superb steam railway can be found at www.gecp.asso.fr

## F3 – Train des Merveilles

This is a route from Nice on France's Mediterreanean coast up the Roya valley into the Italian Alps through the Col de Tende. The destination is Cuneo and is reached through the Italian town of Limone-Piemont. It was in 1856 that the French sought an international route north from Nice into Italy. As it turned out it was the Italian authorities who first began construction in 1879. However, there were many delays as the military authorities from both countries were sceptical about the national security implications of building the railway. Notwithstanding, in 1895, the French Government gave approval for the work to re-commence. Ironically, the first train to arrive in 1913 at Tende-Val-des-Merveilles station was from Italy! The onset of World War I brought the construction work to a halt. It was not re-started until 1920, a full two years after the war had ended. In 1928, the line was formally opened, 72 years after the original idea had first been mooted! It was electrified for part of its route in Italy (between Limone and Cuneo) in 1935. However, the early successes of the railway were not long-lived. Unfortunately, in World War II, 75 per cent of the line was destroyed in the fighting - perhaps the military

Train des Merveilles - SNCF-TER railcar No. 76583 approaches St Dalmas de Tende station on 13th May, 2006. *Author*

authorities had found a better way to frustrate the railway! After the end of hostilities, the French side of the line was re-built and re-opened to traffic in 1947, but it took another 22 years before the Italian section was re-established. The route heads north-east from Nice through the longest railway tunnel in France (5,938 m) under the Col de Braus to Breil-sur-Roya where it joins the line coming in from the Italian town of Ventimiglia in the south-east. Consequently, this single track line, not electrified before Limone, carries both French and Italian-liveried trains beyond Breil-sur-Roya over the border (*see entry I1*). At Breil-sur-Roya is the Ecomusée des Transport et des Techniques, a mainly outdoor museum safeguarding retired SNCF electric locomotives and other interesting items of French railway history. The route offers outstanding mountainous scenery as can be seen from the train. On one very special part of its journey above Breil-sur-Roya, the train climbs up the mountain heights in three separate 360º spirals known in French as *boucles* which travel sometimes in the open, other times in galleries or through long tunnels. The official SNCF website is www.trainstouristiques-ter.com Another helpful and interesting website is www.beyond.fr/travel/railcuneo.html

### F4 – Train des Alpages

This SNCF-RER route starts out at Marseille-St Charles and travels up the Durance valley to Aspres-sur-Buëch and Veynes Devoluy before turning eastwards for Gap and heading on to its final destination, Briançon. It is a long journey - 260 km - and normally takes just over four hours. This route is a standard SNCF year-round service. During winter, the latter part of the route is used by nightly 'Ski-Specials' from Paris to Briançon. However, on Saturdays only, in July and August, SNCF-TER operates another 'special' leaving Marseille at 06.00 and arriving back at 21.33 with intermediate stops at Aix-en-Provence, Manosque, Sisteron, Montdauphin and

SNCF-TER railcar No. 81635 approaches Gap station on 27th August, 2008. *Author*

L'Argentière. The return ticket price is special too at €20 (2009) for an adult return ticket and half price for children (4-12 years). The countryside beyond Aix-en-Provence following the Durance river is truly a delight to behold. The river, whose source is in the ski resort of Montgenèvre near Briançon in the south-western Cottian Alps, is in fact a 324 km-long tributary of the River Rhône which it joins near Avignon. The main tributaries of the Durance are the Bléone and the Verdon. Whilst it is some distance from the route of this railway, if travelling by car in the area, the Verdon Gorge, east of Gap, should not be missed. The gorge, known as France's 'Grand Canyon', is 20 km long and more than 300 m deep. The views from the top of the gorge are truly breath-taking but definitely are not for those with a fear of heights. The alpine scenery really begins to show after Gap, the capital of the Hautes-Alpes department. Next comes Embrun, a town located at the eastern end of the largest man-made lake in Europe, Lac de Serre-Ponco. It is 30 km long and up to 3 km wide. The lake, fed by the Durance and Ubaye rivers, supports 16 hydroelectric plants and provides irrigation for 1,500 sq. km of nearby land. Damming of the rivers and the valley to form the lake began in 1955 with the objective of controlling the rivers' water flow. There has been a long history of the rivers being the cause of local disastrous floods. The lake was first proposed in 1895 but work did not begin for many decades; indeed, it was not completed until 1961. As one passes by on the train one cannot fail to be impressed, in any season of the year, with the magnificent scene as high mountains plunge into the clear turquoise blue waters below. On from Embrun, the village of Montdauphin is passed before reaching L'Argentière which at one time had its own silver mine, hence its name. The end of the line is reached at Briançon, a fortress town having the reputation as being the highest town in Europe. It is listed as a UNESCO World Heritage site and whilst the town has much to offer it does tend to be overrun with tourists at any time of the year. More information about Train des Alpages specials can be obtained from the website www.trainstouristiques-ter.com/train_alpage.htm

## F5 – Crest to Aspres-sur-Buëch and Veynes Devoluy

The railway line from Livron in the Rhône valley takes the traveller to the town of Crest, south-east of Valence in the department of the Drôme. It is situated in the foothills of the Alps. From far away, the town can be seen pinpointed by its distinctive monument, the Crest Tower. This is all that remains of the 11th century castle which was completely destroyed in the 17th century. However, the tower did find a new role as a State Prison for a while. Mulberry bushes abound locally hinting, quite rightly, that silk-worm breeding and silk-spinning perhaps are important local activities. The manufacture of woollens, paper, leather and cement are also important industries in the area. There is also a trade in highly prized truffles, the so-called 'diamond of the kitchen'. Ten miles south-east of Crest lies the picturesque Forest of Saon. Travelling east for 38 km and hugging the valley of the River Drôme the line reaches the small town of Die, famous for its sparkling wine, Clairette de Die. A festival celebrating wine and local gastronomy is held here in early September each year. Travelling for a further 60 km one arrives at Aspres-sur-Buëch, a junction of four railway routes - the one just described, one north to Grenoble (Train des Alpes – *see next entry*) one to the south from Sisteron (Train des Alpages – *see previous entry*) and finally one to the east to Briançon, also part of the Train des Alpages route. However, Aspres-sur-Buëch is not the principal railway centre of the region, that honour belongs to Veynes Devoluy, 8 km to the east. Veynes is a small town but boasts a long railway history as clearly indicated by the size of the now empty marshalling yards next to the station. One can discover more by visiting the Cheminot Veynois Ecomusée in the town. This museum, housed in an 18th century mansion, celebrates the railway history and local traditions of Veynes and its surrounding areas. Veynes was the birthplace of the 19th century engineer Adrien Ruelle. Ruelle (1815–1887) known locally as *l'étoile de Veynes* (en. Star of Veynes) became a director of

Passengers boarding a midday service at Luc en Diois station *en route* to Aspres-sur-Buëch on 27th August, 2008.    *Author*

Train des Alpes – SNCF-TER railcar crosses the viaduct over the River Sareymonde near La Croix Haute on 28th August, 2008.

*Author*

the Compagnie des Chemins de Fer de Paris à Lyon et à la Méditerranée (PLM) and was instrumental in the design and construction of many railway lines in the Alps. In addition, he built homes and other facilities for railway workers. At Veynes he built the locomotive depot which included a *rotonde* (en. roundhouse). He entered politics and had become a regional councillor by the time the first train entered Veynes in 1875. Veynes benefits from an exceptional climate enjoying more than 300 days of sunshine each year. This has led to a spin-off benefit for the town in that it has now become a pioneering location for the development of solar technology.

## F6 – Le Train des Alpes

Le Train des Alpes is the name of the route between Aspres-sur-Buëch and Grenoble, 110 km away. The line was first proposed in 1856 and built between 1870 and 1880. The geographical and geological characteristics of the area presented many problems requiring the construction of 27 tunnels varying in length between 50 m and 1,175 m, 15 viaducts from 48 m to 285 m high and five bridges between 30 m and 60 m high. The area north of Gap and south of Grenoble is one of France's nine national parks – Parc national des Écrins. It rises to 4,102 m (13,458 ft) at the Barre des Ecrins, the most southerly alpine peak above 4,000 m in Europe. The park covers 918 sq. km of high mountainous areas, with many high peaks, glaciers fields and valleys, alpine pastures and sub-alpine woodlands and lakes. Also touching this route is the Park Natural Regional du Vercors lying to the north and west. The Vercors is a plateau in the departments of Isère and Drôme and is one of the ranges which forms the French Prealps. It lies west of the Dauphiné Alps, from which it is separated by the Drac and Isère rivers. It offers several popular resorts for cross-country and down-hill skiing. The largest resort is Villard-de-Lans. The cliffs on its eastern edge face Grenoble the largest city in the Alps and

capital of the Isère department. Grenoble is also surrounded by other mountain ranges. To the north is the Chartreuse, famous for the liquor produced by the Carthusian monks, and, to the east, the Belledonne range. The route from Aspres-sur-Buëch passes through the villages of Lus-La-Croix Haute, Clelles-Mens, Monestier de Clermont and Vif before arriving at Grenoble. Travelling from south to north the mountains to west include Le Jocou (2,056 m), Mont Barral (1,908 m), the flat-topped Mont Aiguille (2,097 m), Grand Veymont (2,341 m) and La Grand Moucherolle (2,284 m) and to the east Grand Ferrand (2,761 m) and the highest on the route L'Obiou (2,793 m). Not far from Vif is St Georges-de-Commiers from where the Chemin de Fer de la Mure operates (*see next entry*). For more information visit the SNCF website which is very helpfully produced in English www.trainstouristiques-ter.com/train_alpes_anglais.htm

## F7 – Chemin de Fer de la Mure

The line from St Georges-de-Commiers (alt. 316 m) to La Mure (alt. 882 m) was originally built in 1888 as part of a 114 km line towards Gap. Its prime function was to transport coal from the local pits at La Mure up to St Georges-de-Commiers for onward transportation to Grenoble and elsewhere. In its early days as many as 12 Fives-Lille steam locomotives were used, each hauling 10 fully loaded wagons. However, between 1903 and 1911 the railway embarked upon a programme of electrification which allowed newly acquired Swiss-Franco electric locomotives to double the previous haulage capacity. After the end of World War II, the use of the line decreased in favour of road transport. In 1950, passenger traffic on the line stopped and goods transport ceased two years later. The conveyance of the mined anthracite by rail continued until 1988 but that was then transferred to the road. The mines eventually closed in 1997. Happily, tourism has given the railway a

Chemin de Fer de la Mure locomotive No. 9 hauls a mid-afternoon service across a viaduct near La Motte-St-Martin heading for La Mure on 23rd August, 2005.

*Author*

new lease of life. Passenger traffic re-commenced in 1988 and today, operated by Veolia Transport, thousands of tourists enjoy the natural beauty of the area and marvel at the achievements of this 120-year-old railway. Said to be one of the most beautiful railway routes in the Alps it claims to be the first electrified railway in the world which is still operating today. The route of the line is an outstanding feat of engineering with 142 *ouvrages d'art* including 18 tunnels and 12 bridges/viaducts. Perhaps the most outstanding structure is the viaduct suspended 150 metres above the gorge at the Monteynard Barrage, a dam which was built to flood the Drac valley. Also worth seeing from the road, rather than the train, are Les Viaducs de Loulla, two viaducts one above the other in the same cutting. Other local attractions include La Mine Image at La Motte d'Aveillans which traces the history of mining in the area and L'Écomusée de l'Abeille (en. bee museum) at the railway station in La Motte d'Aveillans. For more information visit Veolia's website at www.trainlamure.com/pages/en/6/chemin-de-fer-de-la-mure.html

### F8 – Grenoble to Chambéry and to St Pierre d'Albigny

Grenoble, is a modern high-technology city at the foot of Chartreuse Mountains and at the confluence of the Drac and Isère rivers. A double track electrified line (25kV AC) from Grenoble to Chambéry first travels to Gières. Thereafter, only diesel-powered services continue to Montméilan. At Montméilan is a meeting with the electrified track (1500V DC) from Chambéry which continues to St Pierre d'Albigny. From there it divides, one the Ligne de la Tarentaise to Albertville and Bourg St Maurice (*see entry F11*) and the other the Ligne de la Maurienne to Modane (*see entry F12*). For the author this is one of the most attractive railway routes in this region. Travelling up the open and wide Isère river valley – part of Hannibal's route in 218 BC from Spain to Italy - the views are

superb with the Chartreuse mountains on the left and the Bauge mountains ahead and to the right. Chambéry, a town of about 60,000 inhabitants, is the capital of the Savoie department. Chambéry was founded at the crossroads of ancient routes from Dauphiné, Burgundy, Switzerland and Italy; it was not surprising therefore that when the railways came to the region it became an important hub in France's rail network. Indeed, the *rotonde* is still fully operational there. Another famous landmark in the city is the Fontaine des Éléphants, built not to celebrate Hannibal's exploits but to commemorate those of Benoît de Boigne, a famous French general, who won many victories in the early part of the 19th century in India. Lac du Bourget, near to Chambéry, is France's largest (18 km by 3½ km) and deepest (145 m) natural lake.

### F9 – Grenoble to St André-le-Gaz and on to Chambéry

The route from Grenoble to St André-le-Gaz, a small town of under 2,000 inhabitants, is a double-tracked electrified main line carrying inter-city services via Moirans and Voiron ultimately destined for Lyon. At St André-le-Gaz the line meets the main line from the city of Lyon which arrives there via Lyon's TGV station, followed by the townships of Bourgoin-Jallieu and La Tour-du-Pin. At St André-le-Gaz a single track line goes to Chambéry. From Chambéry the line continues north to Aix-les-Bains on the shores of Lac du Bourget.

### F10 – St Marcellin to Moirans

This railway line, operating just diesel-powered trains, is a little over 40 km long. It was single-tracked but in 2008 work began to double it all the way to Romans-sur-Isère (famous for its production of shoes) a distance of 72 km. The beautiful valley of the

Local service train hauled by No. 26591 approaches Grenoble station on 22nd June, 2008.

*Author*

Train hauled by locomotive No. 522214 near St André le Gaz heading for Le Pont-de-Beauvoison and Chambéry on 20th June, 2008.

*Author*

Near Moirans station on 19th June, 2008, RFF work in progress to develop double track. *Author*

Isère river once again shapes the direction of the route. The growing of walnuts is a huge industry in this area as evidenced by the seemingly endless groves.

## F11 – Ligne de la Tarentaise

Ligne de la Tarentaise is the name of the route from St Pierre d'Albigny to Bourg St Maurice via Albertville, Moutiers-Salins and Aime-la-Plagne. The total distance covered by this single-tracked railway is 80 km. The track parallels the River Isére all the way and almost to its source in the Savoie Alps. The line was built by the PLM company over a period of 34 years. The section from St Pierre d'Albigny to Albertville opened in October 1879, from Albertville to Moutiers in June 1893 and the final section to Bourg St Maurice in November 1913. Albertville was the host of the Winter Olympics in 1992. Prior to that event, in the late 1980s, a programme of modernisation was implemented on the line including electrification and improved signalling. Today, the line carries local TER (Transport Express Régional) services, fast TGV trains conveying winter sports enthusiasts direct from Paris in just less than five hours, and, of course, and freight. On Saturdays in winter it is not unusual to see a Eurostar train arriving in Bourg St Maurice eight hours after it has left London. Albertville, in the Savoie department, is on the River Arly close to the confluence with the River Isère. It is a relatively young town having been founded in 1836 by the King of Sardinia, Charles Albert, albeit there are some 14th century buildings in one of its older quarters, Conflans. Its population is under 20,000 but this is bolstered significantly by visitors especially during the winter months. Nearby to this railway are the mountain ranges of the Bauges with 14 summits of 2,000 m or over, the Beaufortain which hosts the annual *Pierra Menta* ski touring competition, a 'must-do' for the athletic, and the Vanoise National Park the first in France to be so designated in

Gare d'Albertville on 21st June, 2008. *Author*

Aerial view taken on 7th March, 2009 of Modane station with a TGV awaiting departure on the Ligne de Maurienne. *Author*

1963. Bourg St Maurice, often shortened to Bourg, is the largest town in the Tarentaise valley. Bourg is part of the *Paradiski* ski-area offering uninterrupted skiing in Les Arcs, Peisey-Vallandry and La Plagne which collectively offer over 400 km of pistes. The 'Vanoise Express', a double-decker cable car and the only one in the world that has a capacity for over 200 people, has linked these areas since 2003. Unfortunately, it has had an unsatisfactory recent history. Because of safety inspections at the end of 2007, the service was closed for the rest of that winter season, effectively shutting down the Paradiski and its economy. It has since re-opened. Bourg St Maurice is the end of the line, the only route into nearby Italy (15 km as the crow flies) being by road over a twisting 28 km to the (Little) St Bernard Pass and on to Aosta.

### F12 – Ligne de la Maurienne

The Ligne de la Maurienne route, also known as the Mont Cenis route, follows the River Arc for all of the way from St Pierre d'Albigny to Modane on the Italian border. It was built in the mid-19th century with the section from St Pierre d'Albigny to St Jean de Maurienne opened in October 1856. This was followed by a section further up the line to St Michel de Maurienne in March 1862 and the final connection to Modane and into Italy to Bussoleno in October 1871. The entry into Italy was achieved by the building of a tunnel under the Pointe du Fréjus (2,932 m) and the Col de Fréjus (2,542 m). As a matter of interest, the tunnel did not produce the first rail crossing. Between 1868 and 1871, there was a railroad, known as 'The Devil's Ladder', over the pass, which was used primarily to transport mail from Britain on its way to India! The construction of the tunnel began from the Italian side (Bardonecchia) in August 1857 and from French side (Modane) in December the same year. The two sides eventually met 13 years later. Originally, it had been thought that the breakthrough would take as long as 25 years but

this was much reduced with the invention of the pneumatic drill and later the use of a new explosive, Alfred Nobel's 'dynamite'. In 1882, the Gotthard Rail Tunnel and in 1906 the Simplon Tunnel were built using similar techniques and benefiting from the Fréjus experience. The Fréjus rail tunnel was originally 12.8 km in length but in 1881 was extended to 13.7 km with the construction of a greater reinforced entrance on the French side. At the time of its opening in September 1871 it was the world's longest tunnel having taken this accolade from the Standedge tunnels (5.1 km) under the Lancashire/Yorkshire Pennines in England. Between 1925 and 1930 the Maurienne line was electrified using a third rail carrying 1500V DC but in 1976 whilst the voltage was maintained this was changed to an overhead supply. An excellent article on the building of the Mont Cenis Railway and Tunnel was published in *Harper's New Monthly Magazine* in July 1871. It can be read on website at www.catskillarchive.com/rrextra/mrcenis.html

Today there are plans for the construction of a new Lyon-Turin route to improve the flow of freight between France and Italy. At present (2009) some 130 million tonnes of freight are moved each year through the southern Aps. The Fréjus/Mont Cenis tunnel currently carries 10 million tonnes and is expected to reach its maximum capacity by 2017. The project jointly managed by France's Reseau Ferré de France (RFF) and Italy's Rete Ferroviaria Italiana (RFI) will include the building of a 53.1 km long tunnel. The total cost of the project is estimated to be €6.3 billion.

### F13 – Aix-les-Bains to St Gervais-les-Bains (Le Fayet)

A little over 9 km north of Chambéry, by rail or road, one arrives at Aix-les-Bains. The town, standing at an altitude of 250 m, is situated on the eastern shore of Lac du Bourget, France's largest natural lake. The Tour de L'Angle Est (1,562 m) overlooks the town and lake. The town lies in the attractive hilly Bugey countryside

A TGV bound for Annecy crosses a small river in the Gorges du Fier near Chavanod on 28th August, 2008.

*Author*

which forms part of the Prealps. Aix-les Bains traces much of its history to the Roman occupation of France. Here they discovered springs which they developed for thermal baths. These baths, fed by sulphur-impregnated water, maintain temperatures between 43 and 45ºC (109-113ºF). Today, they are very popular attracting thousands of visitors every year to take the waters both for drinking and for hydrotherapy. Care has to be taken though, for it is said that the water can be hot enough to scald the skin. The line from Chambéry to Aix-les-Bains is double-tracked and electrified (1500V DC). At Aix-les-Bains the line splits with one route continuing north alongside the lake to Culoz. There it further divides with one line going to Amberieu-sur-Bugey and the other to the industrial town of Bellegarde and on to Geneva (*see next entry*). Back in Aix the other divided line is single-tracked (25kV AC) which travels north to Albens and then north-east to Annecy and La Roche-sur-Foron before turning south-east to St Gervais-les-Bains. Annecy

(population 52,000) is a city 35 km south of Geneva and lies at the northern end of Lake Annecy, a very popular holiday resort, especially for weekenders and day-trippers from Lyon. In design, the town is like a small version of Venice with the river (Thiou), small canals and streams running through. Standing in these waterways is one of the most photographed monuments in the city (and maybe all of France) the 12th century Palais de l'Isle, sometimes referred to as the 'Old Prison'. From Annecy, the railway continues to the popular French ski resort of Cluses, in the Arve valley. Cluses may be well known to anglers for located in the town is the Mitchell Company whose claim to fame was in introducing the first spinning reel to aid game fishing. The next main station is Sallanches-Combloux-Megève, again serving important ski resorts, before reaching St Gervais-les-Bains the starting point of the Mont Blanc Express (*see entry F18*) and at Le Fayet the departure station for the Tramway du Mont Blanc (*see entry F19*).

## F14 – Aix-les-Bains to Bellegarde

Travelling north from Aix-les-Bains the railway hugs the eastern shore of Lac du Bourget before reaching Culoz (population 2,914) which lies on the River Rhône and very close to the first foothills of the Alps. The town is dominated by the Grand Colombier (1,534 m) which is the highest summit at the southern end of the Jura Mountains. Culoz is an important and busy railway hub. Heading north from Culoz the line travels through pleasant rolling countryside following for the entire journey the River Rhône before arriving in Bellegarde in the department of Ain. On this 35 km-long route is the attractive town of Seyssel. Bellegarde-sur-Valserine, to give the full name of this industrial town of 15,000 inhabitants, is located at the meeting of the rivers Valserine and Rhône.

## F15 – Bellegarde to Annemasse

Shortly after Bellegarde, the route splits at Longeray-Léaz with the double-tracked line (1500V DC) continuing to Geneva and a single-tracked secondary line, with the benefit of a 25kV AC overhead power supply, travelling 40 km to Annemasse on the Franco-Swiss border. Given its border location Annemasse is a popular commercial centre especially with the Swiss (resident outside the European Community) coming in to buy food, wine and other commodities. The town stands on the Arve river, a tributary of the Rhône, and has the mountains of Salève (1,300 m) and Voirons (1,450 m) as its neighbours.

## F16 – Annemasse to Evian-les Bains

Lake Geneva is shared by Switzerland and France. The lake is known to the French as Lac Léman. In terms of surface area, it is the second largest freshwater lake in Central Europe. (NB: The largest is Lake Balaton in Hungary.) Switzerland administers 60 per cent of the lake under the jurisdiction of the cantons of Vaud, Geneva, and Valais and 40 per cent by France's Haute-Savoie department. The railway route from Annemasse to the present end of the line at Evian-les-Bains passes through Bons-en-Chablais and Thonon-les-Bains, a total distance of 41 km. For the final part of the journey, the 10 km starting just before Thonon-les-Bains one can enjoy splendid views of the lake. Thonon-les Bains (population *circa* 30,000) is a picturesque French spa town located on the southern shores of the lake and near to the Dranse river. The town is only 19 km from Geneva to which many of the local residents commute. In former times it was the capital of Chablais province and part of the former Duchy of Savoy. Ten kilometres eastwards the railway arrives at Evian-les-Bains (population 7,787) famous for its *Evian* mineral water which, with tourism, is the mainstay of its economy. In July 1938, a conference was convened here by President Franklin D. Roosevelt to discuss the mounting problem of Jewish refugees. Unfortunately, the conference did not pass a resolution condemning the German treatment of Jews which perhaps emboldened Hitler and his cohorts to go on to further monstrous behaviour. Eastwards beyond Evian-les-Bains the path of the former railway to St Gingolph on the Swiss border still exists although no longer in use, but maybe one day! Swiss Federal Railways (SBB) still operate services to St Gingolph from Martigny (*see entry CH 12*).

## F17 – Annemasse to La Roche-sur-Foron

The route from Annemasse to La Roche-sur-Foron at 20 km is a short one but is an important link to the Aix-les-Bains – St Gervais line (*see entry F13*). It is a single track line of secondary status but it is electrified (25kV AC). La Roche-sur-Foron was at one time in its history economically and politically as important as Geneva, which to the visitor nowadays may seem difficult to believe. The modern

Passenger service from Culoz running south to Aix-les-Bains along the banks of Lac du Bourget as seen from the marina at Châtillon on 20th June, 2008.

*Author*

SNCF-TER (Rhône-Alpes) service crossing the River Arve near Annemasse on 29th August, 2008. *Author*

Viaduct crossing the River Dranse at Vongy (between Thonon les-Bains and Evian-les-Bains) on 30th August, 2008. *Author*

No. 23575 leaves La Roche-sur-Foron for Annemasse on 29th August, 2008. *Author*

town is built around a thousand-year-old centre with a rich and varied history. In typically French style bread is still produced in the 200-year-old bakery facing the town's church. The town also claims to be the first in Europe to introduce electric street lighting. There is a popular annual market and fair here in October celebrating St Denis, the town's patron saint.

## F18 – Mont Blanc Express

The Mont-Blanc Express is the name of the train service that runs between St Gervais-les-Bains and Martigny in Switzerland via Vallorcine and Le Châtelard. In 1893, the French Government granted permission to the PLM company to build and operate a railway service between St Gervais-les-Bains and Vallorcine. In June 1899 construction work began on the line, the engineers opting for an electrically-powered metre gauge railway line, traction being driven by an 850 V supply delivered by a third rail. This required the building of two power stations, one at Servoz and the other at Les Chavants. The first section of the route, the 19 km between St Gervais-les-Bains and Chamonix was opened in 1901. Following on the early commercial success of this first section, a second was opened to Argentière. About the same time on the Swiss side of the frontier, a line from Martigny to Le Châtelard was constructed. However, for the two lines to be connected Le Col des Montets (1,461 m) had to be overcome. This was achieved by the building of a 1,883 m-long tunnel which was completed by the end of 1907. The official opening of the full route took place on 1st July, 1908. In 1937, the PLM company, was nationalized and SNCF became became the new operator. Today, over 100 years on, the line continues to serve mainly the tourist industry. Taking advantage of the train, the traveller can alight to explore the magnificent Vallée de Chamonix and the equally attractive Vallée du Trient. Of course, there is Mont Blanc, at 4,807 m Europe's highest peak, which can be explored by using the Tramway du Mont Blanc (*see entry F 19*), the Mer de Glace glacier with the aid of Chemin de Fer de Chamonix au Montenvers (*see entry F20*) and the Le Barrage d'Emosson (*see entry CH2*). For the less energetic, the Mont-Blanc Express is a unique way of exploring the delights of this outstanding area in armchair comfort admiring on the way the Massif du Mont-Blanc with outstanding views of Les Aiguilles d'Argentière, Le Col de Balme and Le Glacier des Bossons. For more information in English, explore the website www.trainstouristiques-ter.com select the Union Jack flag and choose the Rhône-Alpes region followed by the Le Mont Blanc Express.

A 'Mont Blanc Express' sporting its 100-year anniversary livery leaving Chamonix-Mont Blanc for Le Châtelard on 29th August, 2008.
*Author*

## F19 – Tramway du Mont Blanc

Tramway du Mont Blanc is France's highest railway/tramway. The tramway runs from St Gervais-les-Bains - Le Fayet to Le Nid'Aigle (alt. 2,380 m) a distance of 12 km and a rise in altitude of 1,778 metres. Its history goes back to the end of the 19th and the beginning of the 20th centuries. Many ideas were proposed during those times for the building of a system of mechanized transport up Mont Blanc. The original idea of a railway was that of an engineer named Issartier; he wanted to take his route right to the summit where he intended to build a terminus! However, it was Henri Duportal, an engineer who had been responsible for the PLM line from Cluses to Le Fayet, who rose to the challenge. He thought of the idea of building a tramway from Le Fayet to l'Aiguille du Goûter, a location in altitude 1,000 m lower than the summit. As the cost of his proposal was considerably less than that of the competitors, his idea was accepted. Work began on the railway in 1904 with Col de Voza (alt. 1,653 m) attained in 1907, Bellevue (alt. 1,800 m) in 1911, Nid d'Aigle (alt. 2,372 m) in 1912 and finally to the foot of the Glacier de Bionnassay in 1914. Here, it was decided to terminate the tramway and thereafter it was used only for summer working. However, in 1923, the line was opened for the first time in winter with services operating to the Bellevue station. The traction originally used was steam-driven trams but these were replaced in 1956 with three electrically-driven rack and pinion trams (fr. *motrices*) named *Anne*, *Marie* and *Jeanne* after the then owner's three daughters. This tramway is the highest altitude rack and pinion train in France. Nowadays, services operate between mid-December and mid-April and then from mid-June to late September with regular services running every 60 to 90 minutes. It is estimated that more than 20,000 people ascend the mountain every year. The tramway is operated by the Compagnie du Mont Blanc which also runs the Chemin de Fer de Chamonix au Montenvers (*see next entry*). More detail of services can be found at the website www.compagniedumontblanc.com

## F20 – Chemin de Fer de Chamonix au Montenvers

This tramway and the town where it is located is immensely popular throughout the year, as much in summer for alpine hiking as it is in winter for snow related sports. Indeed the road to Chamonix, the town and its car parks, in the author's experience, are always heavily congested so the best advice is always take the more pleasurable experience of the the Mont Blanc Express train from St Gervais-les-Bains to Chamonix. The Chamonix-Montenvers trams, hauled by electrically self-propelling railcars or sometimes diesel locomotives, travel at speeds of 12-14 kmh and rise in altitude from 1,042 m to 1,913 m. Each train carries between 160 and 200 passengers up gradients which can vary between 11 and 22 per cent. The journey includes a spectacular passage over a viaduct 152 m in length. The line took its first passengers in the summer of 1909 and at that time steam locomotives hauled the carriages with the journey taking about 55 minutes. Incidentally, there is a retired 1923 Swiss-built Winterthur steam locomotive on static display on the platform at Chamonix. Just after the end of World War II, a *grotte* (en. cave) was cut into the famous Mer de Glace (seven kilometres long and France's largest glacier) so that visitors could safely see inside. In 1953, the line became the first electrified rack and cogwheel train (fr. *crémaillère*) in the world. However, it was not until 1993 that the railway first operated winter services. There is only one short suspension of services for maintenance which is usually for the first two weeks of October each year. The railway is operated by the Compagnie du Mont Blanc which also runs the Tramway du Mont Blanc (*see previous entry*). More detail of services can be found at the website www.compagniedumontblanc.com

The driver descending from Tramway du Mont Blanc's *Anne* and caught 'mid-flight' on 24th August, 2005 at Le Fayet station.

*Author*

CF de Chamonix au Montenvers No. 53 climbing out of Chamonix station on 30th August, 2008. Mont Blanc provides the backdrop.

*Caroline Jones*

# Italy

## Introduction

The southern boundary of the Alps from France to the east takes us into Italy. The Italian Alps are bordered to the north by Switzerland and Austria and further east by Slovenia, formerly part of Yugoslavia.

The prime road crossings into the Italian Alps from its neighbouring countries are from France by the Mont Blanc and Fréjus tunnels; the Colle di Pic St Bernardo (small) pass; from Moutiers to Courmayeur; from Briançon towards Turin (Torino) via Oulx; and, from Nice towards Cuneo via the Colle di Tenda.

The Italian Alps, moving from west to east, are entered from Switzerland, Austria and Slovenia (Slovenija).

From Switzerland the first access is by way of the Gran St Bernardo pass and the nearby tunnel from Martigny to Aosta; from Brig to Domodossola via the Simplon Pass; each side of Lake Maggiore, i.e. from Locarno to Verbania and Bellinzona to Como; the Splügen Pass to Chiavenna; and, finally, Chiavenna is also reached through Soglio from St Moritz. The latter is also the departure point for the crossing to Tirano via the Piz Bernina pass.

From Austria there are four prime road routes into the Alps. The first in the west is from Landeck to St Valentino alla Muta via Passo di Rosia; from Sölden to Merano via the Passo del Rombo and down the Val Passinia; the famous Brenner (it. Brennero) Pass taking traffic from Innsbruck to Bolzano/Bozen; and, finally, from Lienz to Dobbiaco-Toblach in the Dolomites.

Slovenia (SLO) enjoys two major and four minor routes into the Italian Alps. To the north is the crossing from Jesenice to Tarvisio via Ratece and to the south is the crossing from near Nova Gorica (SLO) to Gorizia heading for Udine. There is also a minor border crossing near Nova Gorica. The minor routes are in the north over the Passo di Predil, i.e. from Bovec (SLO) to Tarvisio; one very small route near Slovenia's Zaga; and, finally, in from Robic (SLO) to Cividale.

Six of Italy's 20 regions engage parts of the Italian Alps: Aosta Valley, Piedmont, Lombardy, Veneto, Trentino-Alto Adige and Friuli Venezia Giulia.

The **Aosta Valley**, in the north-east corner of Italy with its principal town of Courmayeur provides some of the best and perhaps most exciting skiing and winter sports activity in the Alps. The scenery, as elsewhere in the Alps, is truly outstanding especially the Gran Paradiso, Monte Bianco, Monte Rosa and Matterhorn mountains.

**Piedmont** which literally means 'foot of the mountain' is a most apt title. It is the second largest administrative region, after Sicily, and is located in the north-west of the country with its alpine range running from north to south towards the Mediterranean and along the French border. The region's capital is Turin located on the plain. The largest Alpine towns are Cuneo, north of Nice, and Sestriere to the east of France's Briançon. Piedmont hosts the source of Italy's largest river, the Po. There is a considerable number of national and regional parks in the area, 56 in fact, of which perhaps the most famous is the Gran Paradiso.

Approximately one sixth of Italy's population lives in the region of **Lombardy**. Its capital city is Milan (Milano). The region comprises a mix of mountains, lakes and plains. The Alpine zone includes the Lepontine and Rhaetian Alps, with the Piz Bernina at 4,049 m above sea level, the Bergamo Alps, the Ortles and the Adamello massifs. There is also an area of Alpine foothills with the main summits being the Grigna (2,410 m), Resegone (1,875 m) and Presolana (2,521 m). Glaciers formed the origins of the great lakes of Lombardy region. Travelling from west to east they are Lake Maggiore, Lake Lugano of which the major part is in Switzerland, Lake Como, Lake Iseo, Lake Idro, and, of course, Lake Garda which is the largest of all in Italy.

**Veneto** is one of the wealthiest and most industrialized regions of Italy. It also happens to be the most visited region in the whole of Italy with over 60 million tourists every year, perhaps not surprising given that Venice is its capital. The northern part of the region, about 29 per cent, is in the alpine zone including the Carnic Alps (highest peaks being Coglians at 2,780 m and Kellerwand at 2,775 m), the eastern Dolomites and the Venetian Prealps with (comparitively minor peaks between 700 m and 2,200 m). The Dolomites range contains the highest of Italy's alpine peaks including the famous Marmolada which at 3,342 m is the highest in the region. The Tofane, the Tre Cime di Lavaredo and the Pale di San Martino are also well-known ranges. Several important rivers flow through the region such as the Po, the Adige, the Brenta, the Bacchiglione, the Livenza, the Piave, and the Tagliamento. Wine is a common product of this region; for example, white wines such as Garda Classico, Recioto di Soave and Vivenza and red wines of Bardolino, Colli di Coneglliano and Valpolicella.

**Trentino-Alto Adige** in north-eastern Italy comprises two provinces, the Trento and Bolzano/Bozen. The region was originally part of the Austro-Hungarian Empire until it was ceded to Italy in 1919 after the end of World War I. Given its history, the German language, as well as Italian, is commonly spoken in the area. The region covers 13,619 sq. km and is extremely mountainous embracing a large part of the Dolomites with their jagged peaks, and the southern Alps. It also has the lowest international crossing of the Alps at the Brenner Pass (alt. 1,371 m) located in the far north of the region on the border with Austria. Wine, and good quality at that, is also a popular product of the region, especially up the main valley from Verona towards Austria where the vineyards seem never ending. It is said that there are 40 vines for every inhabitant!

**Friuli Venezia Giulia** is located in the far north-east corner of Italy. Its capital is Trieste on the Adriatic coast which happens to be outside the Alpine range. It is one of five regions in Italy which enjoys special status in respect of their legislation, administration and economy. This means they are allowed to keep 60 per cent of all taxes levied but at a cost of having to finance their own healthcare, education and local government institutions. The alpine ranges in this region are the Friulian Dolomites with the highest peaks being the Cima dei Preti (2,703 m), the Duranno (2,652 m) and the Cridola (2,580 m); the Carnic Alps, highest peaks being Peralba (2,691 m) and Bìvera (2,474 m) as well as Coglians (2,780 m); and, the Julian Alps, with the Jôf Fuârt (2,666 m), the Jôf di Montasio (2,754 m), Mangart (2,677 m) and the Canin (2,587 m). Some way from Trieste is Udine the capital of the Friuli province and closest city in this region to the Alps. Wine again is a important local product.

The 10 principal cross-border railway routes are from Nice to Cuneo via Colle di Tenda; Modane to Oulx via the Fréjus railway tunnel; Martigny to Aosta via the St Bernard tunnel; the Simplon tunnel from Brig to Domoddosola; Bellinzona to Domodossola; Cadenazzo to Luino; St Moritz to Tirano; the Brenner Pass crossing; Lienz to Dobbiaco-Toblach; and, finally, Arnoldstein to Tarvisio-Boscoverde. There are further 19 railway routes in the Italian Alps.

Italy, in the main, utilizes a 3000V DC power supply for its electrically-driven trains.

### The Railways

### I1 – Ventimiglia to Cuneo

France's Train des Merveilles (*see entry F3*) shares journeys with Italian Railways (FS-Trenitalia) on this route. Diesel-powered trains leave Ventimiglia in Liguria and travel north-west to Olivetta San Michele before crossing the border near Fanghetto into France. The line continues past Piene-Basse where it runs close to the SNCF-TER line for about 3 km before they come together just south of Breil-sur-Roya. The shared line then continues climbing up the steep-sided Roya valley running close to France's D6204 road which is helpful to visitors by car to view the route of the line and

FS Trenitalia passenger service from Cuneo descending the Gorges de Bergue (in France) towards Breil-sur-Roya and Ventimiglia on 13th May, 2006. The train is crossing the D6204 road but note the gallery above the locomotive which is part of the *boucle* being negotiated at this point on the line, north of Fontan. *Author*

marvel at its construction. Just after the village of Fontan the line cuts west and begins its first 360º loop (*boucle,* as the French call it) three-quarters of which is in a tunnel. Continuing for a further 3 km the line snakes its way up, sometimes in the open alongside or crossing the road, sometimes in open-sided galleries and at other times through tunnels. On reaching the village of St Dalmas-de-Tende the line cuts east and begins its second full loop, all in a tunnel, before emerging briefly before more tunnels one of which bypasses the village of Tende. Two kilometres north of Tende, the line again cuts east for its third and final full loop in France the completion of which is not seen as it continues through a tunnel towards the Franco-Italian border. Just before the border, the line emerges into the open and runs near to the road for about a kilometre before disappearing again into a tunnel under the Col de Tende (1,870 m). This is the last time on this route trains can be seen in France. The Col de Tende rail tunnel, which is 8.1 km long, was opened in 1898, 16 years after the 3.2 km road tunnel had been opened. The line enters into Italy near to Limone Piemonte. After a further 7 km, just before the village of Vernante, it turns west and undertakes the only full loop on the Italian side of the border, three-quarters of which is hidden in a tunnel. The line continues north to Borgo San Dalmazzo (population *circa* 12,000) before reaching Cuneo. This railway is single track for its entire route and is not electrified apart from the section in Italy between Limone Piemonte and Cuneo. The railway divides at Cuneo with the electrified route carrying on to Fossano. There are two other lines, both diesel operated, one to Busca and the other to Mondovi. Cuneo is a large 12th century town (population 55,000) and is the capital of the Cuneo province which is the third largest province in Italy. If visiting the town, be sure to taste the local speciality *Cuneesi al rhum*, these are chocolates with a unique rum-based filling - delicious!

## I2 – Bardonecchia to Turin

France's Ligne de la Maurienne (*see entry F12*) enters the 13.7 km-long Fréjus rail tunnel at Modane and emerges into Italy close to the small town of Bardonecchia (population 3,000). Bardonecchia, at an altitude of 1,312 m, is located at the meeting point of four valleys and is surrounded by mountains, many whose peaks exceed 3,000 m. The area is popular for winter sports, indeed, it hosted the snowboarding events in the the 2006 Winter Olympics which were centred on Turin. It is possible to access the town by road from France (Modane) by the parallel Fréjus road toll tunnel. The route of the double-tracked electrified main line railway to Turin, 94 km away, is down the stunning Susa valley with the sheer beauty of the Bosco de Salbertrand National Park and the Parco Naturale Orsiera Rocciavrè. Beyond Avigliana the valley widens and the scenery becomes less attractive as one approaches first the large town of Rivoli and then the bustling city of Turin. Whilst many associate the city with its football teams, Juventus FC and Torino FC, it is important economically, third overall in Italy after Milan and Rome. It is the headquarters of Fiat, Lancia and Alfa Romeo car manufacturers and is often referred to as the 'Detroit of Italy'! Travelling east from Turin is the inter-city line to Milan. The 98 km section of this route to Novara is already designated a high speed line with a further 50 km to be developed to Milan and later to be extended to Verona. Turin has two main railway stations. Construction on the Porta Nuova station, third busiest in Italy, began in 1861 and was completed and opened in 1868 although it was not officially inaugurated until February 2009! The departure area of the station is a sight to behold with frescoes depicting 135 Italian cities and their distances from Turin. The second station in size and importance is the Porta Susa which was built in 1868 as Turin expanded its boundaries westward. Today, the station is undergoing major development with the intention of it becoming Turin's main terminus in 2011. Turin also recently opened its first subway system with Linea 1 (9.6 km) of the Metropolitana di Torino.

Salbertrand station, north-east of Oulx on 7th March, 2009 with a FS passenger service hauled by locomotive No. E633.063. *Author*

FS Trenitalia service from Turin heading for Torre Pellice on 30th September, 2008. *Author*

## I3 – Turin to Torre Pellice

There are three railway routes into the Alps from Turin. Torre Pellice (population 4,500) lies 54 km west-south-west from Turin and is reached on an electrified single track line through the townships of Airasca and Pinerolo. The line terminates at Torre Pellice which is the doorway to the Pellice Valley in Piedmont's Cozie Alps. The valley is about 20 km in length and takes its name from its river, the Pellice, which runs its length. Further up the valley are the villages of Villar Pellice, Bobbio Pellice, and Villanova. Most of the peaks are in excess of 2,500 m, the highest being Monte Granero (3,098 m). The road through the valley terminates at Villanova and from where there are a series of footpaths which run a further 4 or 5 km into France and the Queyras National Park. Whilst there are plenty of outdoor pursuits to follow in the area, for example, high and low level hiking, rock climbing, skiing, horse riding, mountain biking, hunting and fishing, it is not highly developed for the tourist, thus retaining its quiet and unspoilt character. In May 2008 floods hit the valley causing much damage but, thankfully, no death or serious injury.

## I4 – Ferrovia Torino-Ceres

Ferrovia Torino-Ceres, also known as Torino-Valli di Lanzo, is operated by the the Turin Transport Group (GTT). Trains depart the city's Torino-Dora station and pass through the huge Fiat complex before crossing the motorway and into the Parco Chic Mendes eventually reaching Turin's airport. The line then skirts to the west the Parco Regionale la Mandria. The line continues to Ciriè, a town which, in spite of its relative small size (population 18,178) is designated as a 'city'; it has long history with many interesting old buildings and churches. It is also a notable centre of local culture. The line continues north following the river known as the Stura di Lanzo which traces its source to the melting snows of the Graain Alps near Ceres. The river is 65 km in length eventually joining the River Po in Turin. The Lanzo is famous for its whitewater rafting offering challenges both to beginners and the experienced with its many narrow gorges and several lengths of seriously fast rapids. Germagnano, up until November 2008, was the terminus of the line; however, that has now changed with the re-opening of the rail service to Ceres using a refurbished Aln 668 diesel railcar. (These railcars, of which there were 787 built between 1954 and 1983 were a product of Fiat Ferroviaria.) The restored service only runs to and from Ceres and Germagnano; it is necessary, therefore, to change at the latter station, there being no direct trains from Turin.

## I5 – Ferrovia Canavesana

The Ferrovia Canavesana is a 74 km railway line which was constructed in 1856 to connect Turin (Settimo Torinese) with Pont Canavese via the townships of Volpiano, San Benigno Canavese, Bosconero, Feletto, Rivarolo Canavese, Favria, Salassa, Valperga and Cuorgnè. Pont Canavese, a town of many bridges on the River Orco, has a population of just fewer than 4,000. There is much to

A passenger service operated by the Turin Transport Group (TTG) on 30th September, 2008 approaches Balangero station. *Author*

TTG's railcar No. ALn 668 907 ST heads for Turin having just left Cuorgnè station on 30th September, 2008. *Author*

see and do in the area both culturally and athletically. It is a popular centre for summer hiking and climbing as well as for winter sports. One frequently used route from the town, for example, is the hike from Campidaglio (1,110 m) to the Punta Arbella peak (1,879 m). It is from the slopes of this mountain that the Orco is sourced. From the summit one has marvellous views of the Canavese plain and the mountains of Valli Orco e Soana which is part Gran Paradiso National Park.

### I6 – Chivasso to Aosta and Pre St Didier

Taking the train to the Aosta Valley is a splendid alternative to using the car. Aosta railway station is situated close to the cable car station linking the town with the Pila skiing district. Aosta has direct train services to and from Turin's stations of Porta Nuova or Porta Susa, with frequent daily services running about every hour at busy times. The journey takes about two hours. The main railway stations along the Valle d'Aosta line are Pont-Saint-Martin, Verrès and Chatillon-Saint-Vincent, locations which are all connected to neighbouring valleys by local bus services whose operating times generally link with train arrivals and departures. One can also continue the journey by train from the station at Aosta for a further 30 km to the spa town of Pré-Saint-Didier, at the foot of Monte Bianco (Mont Blanc), where the railway terminates. The Aosta Valley, surprisingly perhaps given its altitude, is an important centre for the production of wine. Other local produce includes meat, fruit, and herbs. Incidentally, génépy is a well-known local liqueur distilled from certain herbs collected from the moraines of the glaciers. Famous cheeses also originate here such as Fontina, VDA Formadzo, Gressoney Toma, Salignoun, Rébleque, Broissa, Seras and a variety of goat cheeses.

FS Trenitalia's No. Aln 663 1003/1011 travelling from Novara via Borgmanero to Domodossola seen here north of Premosello-Chiovenda on 22nd September, 2008.                                                                                         *Author*

## I7 – Borgmanero to Domodossola

There is a main line from Milan to Domodossola running alongside Lake Maggiore which is described for part of its journey later (*see entry I10*). However, this secondary route to Domodossola runs to the west of the main line and north from Ornavasso almost in parallel with it. The line, single track and electrified, initially starts out at the large city of Novara (population 190,000) and travels north to Borgmanero where the altitude of the terrain begins to rise as trains head for the alpine mountains. Whilst the main line has Lake Maggiore for company, this line is not to be upstaged for it has the beautiful Lake Orta as neighbour to the left (west) from Bolzano Novarese to the end of the lake at Omegna. Thereafter, it continues to Gravellona Toce at the north-western head of Lake Maggiore and then on to Domodossola following the River Toce. The outstanding Parco Nazionale Val Grande is on the train's right. The total distance covered by this route is 62 km.

## I8 – Romagnano Sesia to Varallo Sesia

Further west from Borgmanero is another secondary line, albeit non-electrified. It runs from the small town of Romagnano Sesia (population 4,000) to the attractive town of Varallo Sesia (population 7,400) 26 km further up and at the end of the line. The River Sesia accompanies the line all the way and the beautiful Monte Fenera National Park is there to admire for almost half of the journey out of the right-hand (east) compartment window. Varallo Sesia has many interesting churches, chapels, museums and 105 m above the town is Sacro Monte di Varallo, one of the most famous pilgrimage sites in Piedmont and which is included on the UNESCO World Heritage list.

Travelling south from Varallo Sesia is FS Trenitalia's No. Aln 663 1015 on 22nd September, 2008 bound for Romagnano Sesia and Novara.
*Author*

SSIF/FART double railcar headed by No. 61 drops down to Masera station before continuing to its final destination of Domodossola on 23rd September, 2008.

*Author*

## I9 – Centovalli

The Centovalli operates services between Domodossola in Piedmont and Locarno in the canton of Ticino in Switzerland, a distance of almost 49 km and a journey time of about 1 hour 45 minutes. The service provider in Italy is Italian Vigezzina operating as Società Subalpina di Imprese Ferroviarie (SSIF) and Ferrovie Autolinee Regionali Ticinesi (FART) in Switzerland. The metre gauge line is an important link between the Simplon line (*see entry I11*) and the Gotthard line. Until the opening of the Furka base tunnel (*see entry - CH26*) in Switzerland this route was the only viable connection between the two Swiss cantons of Ticino and Valais during the winter months. The section in Italy is from the Swiss border which is located between Camedo and Olgia through the Valle Vigezzo to Domodossola, a distance of 35 km. There are 12 stations, 25 bridges/viaducts and 11 tunnels on this section. The maximum gradient is six per cent which is travelled without the benefit of rack/cogwheel assistance and the highest point on this line is at Santa Maria Maggiore (alt. 831 m). The line is electrified at 1350V DC. There are a total of 19 stations in the Italian sector, the first or last being at Ribellasca. The original idea of building the railway goes back to 1898 when the then Mayor of Locarno applied for a licence to operate a rail service. Construction work began in early 1914 but had to be suspended for almost a year when the source of the finance, the Franco-American Bank in Paris, collapsed. Work began again in the spring of 1914 but was short-lived with the onset of World War I. At the end of hostilities there were other priorities so it was not until August 1921 that the building of the railway was re-started. Eighteen months later the Italian and Swiss construction teams met at Santa Maria Maggiore, 13 km into Italy. In November 1923, the railway was officially inaugurated. Today, hourly services operate in both directions during daytime hours. More information about this line can be found in the Swiss chapter of this book (*see entry CH33*). Further detail including timetables, fares, special offers and things to do can be found at www.centovalli.ch

## I10 – Domodossola to Verbania-Pallanza

The main railway route starting out from Milan via the Simplon Tunnel (*see next entry*) to Brig in Switzerland travels through Domodossola. The section of alpine interest is north from the stations serving the Verbania Pallanza, i.e. Mergozzo, Feriolo and Baveno on the shores of Lake Maggiore up to Domodossola. For information, the main line continues south down the western shores of the lake to Seste Calende before running over the plain to Milan. The section to Domodossola shares the valley and destination with the secondary line from Borgmanero (*see entry I7*) following the River Toce with the beautiful Parco Nazionale Val Grande national park first seen to the north then curving round to the east. Main stations on the route are Premosello, Volgogna, Prato and Beura where most of the fast expresses do not stop. There is a considerable quantity of freight carried on the line.

## I11 – The Simplon Rail Tunnel

One of the international routes from Switzerland into Italy is through the Simplon Tunnel. Brig is the main station on the Swiss side and Domodossola the first in Italy. To drive between the two would be over the Simplon Pass (alt. 2,005 m) a distance of 70 km. However, a much quicker alternative is through the Simplon Tunnel on a car-carrying train. Work on the first Simplon tunnel began in 1898 and was opened eight years later jointly by King Victor Emmanuel III of Italy and Ludwig Forrer the President of the Swiss National Council. The tunnel burrowed for almost 20 km under Mount Leone and the Wasenhorn in the Parco Naturale Alpe Veglia. Three thousand workers, mainly Italians, worked on the scheme; 67 were killed in accidents and many others died of disease. There was 2,400 m of rock above the tunnel generating many problems for the workers, for example, heat up to 42°C, a

Headed by locomotive No. E 464.274 an early afternoon service from Domodossola to Milan passes by Beura on 22nd September, 2008.

*Author*

Ponte Boldrini near Iselle di Trasquera is part of a 360º loop just before the entrance to the  Simplon Tunnel. On 23rd September, 2008 a Cisalpino service heads for Brig in Switzerland and beyond.   *Author*

lack of ventilation and water penetration. To address these problems a second tunnel was built parallel to the main tunnel to bring in fresh air and provide a means of escape. Construction was begun from each side of the mountain range and when breakthrough finally came in February 1905 the two halves were found to be out of alignment by a mere 20.2 cm horizontally and 8.7 cm vertically! Given the extraordinary length of the tunnel for that time, a decision was made not to use steam traction but employ what was then a relatively new technology – electrification. The Swiss were well into the use of this technology by this time so it was Brown, Boveri & Cie from Baden who were engaged to install a three-phase power supply of 3,000V DC (the Italian system) using two overhead wires with the track acting as the third conductor. Later, in 1930 the supply was converted to the current system of 15kV AC. Work on what became the second tube of the tunnel began in 1912 and was opened to traffic in 1921. At 19.8 km in length, it was slightly longer than the first tunnel. The opening of this route heralded a whole new chapter in the history of rail travel with the inauguration of the world famous 'Venice–Simplon Orient Express' from London and Paris to Istanbul.

## I12 – Como to Chiasso

A second major rail route between Italy and Switzerland utilising a tunnel, the 15 km long Gotthard north of Biasca (in Switzerland) is the one which starts out from Milan running north to Como on Swiss-Italian border. Trains pass through Monza, famous for its international Formula One racing circuit. From the resort of Como at the southern end of its lake, trains travel a short distance (about 8 km) over the border to Switzerland's Chiasso and from there on to Lugano, Bellinzona and Biasca bound for Zurich, Bern and beyond. The Servizio Ferroviario Regionale (en. Regional Railway Service) connects Como with other major conurbations in Lombardy with services provided by FS-Trenitalia and Ferrovie Nord Milano (FNM). There are two main stations: Como San Giovanni (Trenitalia) and Como Lago (FNM). Albate is another urban station served by Trenitalia trains and there are a further three FNM urban stations, Como Borghi-Università, Como Camerlata and Grandate Breccia. There used to be a rail connection to the important town of Varese from Como but that was abandoned in the 1960s in favour of bus services which are now operated by FNM. Como San Giovanni is the international station on the main line between Milan Centrale and Zurich and Basel. Lake Como is the third largest lake in Italy, after Garda and Maggiore, but it is the deepest at 400 m. Indeed, it is one of the deepest in Europe with half of its depth below sea level. The frequent ferry services on the lake are an important part of the local transport infrastructure. Chiasso, which until 2007 was three

Grafitti - an art form or vandalism? A TILO service awaiting departure for Chiasso in Switzerland from Como San Giovanni station on 29th September, 2008.                                                        *Author*

separate communities, has a population of just over 15,000. Given that Switzerland is not part of the European Community a large part of the town's functions are related to the managing of customs both for road and rail traffic, although some of the border-control aspects have since been transferred to Como.

## I13 – Bergamo to Tirano

Bergamo is a large town in Lombardy 40 km north-east of Milan. The population is 115,000 but this more than doubles when the greater conurbation is taken into account. North of the town the foothills of the Alps rise. From Bergamo an electrified single track secondary line travels for 34 km, through Ponte San Pietro with its remarkable church, to Lecco on the south-east spur of Lake Como.

FS Trenitalia's locomotive No. E 464.100 leads a service across the Adda plain towards Sondrio and Tirano on 29th September, 2008. The mountains of the Parco della Val Masino and Switzerland's Graubunden provide the background.                                *Author*

For much of the journey the line follows the River Adda and the beautiful Parco dell'Adda Nord through which the river flows. Beyond Lecco the railway keeps sight of Lake Como for most of the way as it travels through the large Parco Delle Grigne, 5,000 hectares centered on the notable mountains of the Grigne Massif, before reaching the small town of Colico (population 7,000). From here, a line branches off to Chiavenna (*see next entry*). The line then turns due east still shadowing the River Adda for 81 km before it reaches Sondrio in the heart of the Valtellina, famous today for its skiing, hot spring spas, cheese and wine. The views out of both sides of the train along this stretch and to Tirano are magnificent. There are numerous peaks of over 3,000 m. Travelling for a further 28 km the train reaches its terminus at Tirano, the border town with Switzerland. Unusually for small town of about 9,000 inhabitants it claims ownership of two stations and two independent railways. Of course the journey to here has been by Italy's Ferrovie dello Stato but also arriving literally through the streets of the town is the Bernina Express operated by the Rhaetian Railways (*see entry CH31*).

## I14 – Colico to Chiavenna

Branching north from Colico is the secondary line to Chiavenna, a distance of 30 km. There is an attractive castle here to explore as well as the beautiful Porticato della Collegiata di San Lorenzo with its Romanesque style cloisters. The railway's route from Colico crosses the wide Adda river and travels north-east to Verceia passing the beautiful Mezzola lake which is connected to Lake Como by the Mera river. The Pian di Spagna is a flood plain between the two lakes and is an important area for wintering and migrating water birds. The area with its marvellous alpine peaks is well worth visiting by train or by car. If by car, continuing up the SS36 highway gives the driver and passengers the rewarding experience of the Suretta mountain range before reaching the Passo dello Spluga (Splügen Pass) into Switzerland.

A midday service passes the Mezzola lake at Verceia heading for Chiavenna on 29th September, 2008.

*Author*

The river here flowing into Lake Maggiore forms the boundary between the townships of Germignaga and Luino as seen on 24th September, 2008. The mountains in the background are part of the Valgrande National Park behind Verbania. *Author*

## I15 – Seste Calende to Luino for Bellinzona

On the eastern shores of Lake Maggiore there is another scenic railway. This route travels from Seste Calende north to the Swiss border near Tronzano and then on to Bellinzona in the canton of Ticino. There are some interesting churches in Sesto Calende but of particular architectural note is the 1868-built double iron bridge over the River Ticino at the southern tip of Lake Maggiore. Leaving Sesto Calende, the train heads north on the single track electrified line passing through the Parco Lombardo Valle del Ticino to Ispra. From here the railway accompanies the eastern shores of the lake offering superb views. After 28 km the train reaches the pretty town and port of Laveno-Mombello. Laveno-Mombello operates a frequent ferry service across the lake to the equally attractive but larger town of Verbania. After Laveno-Mombello the train heads north-west but still hugging the shores of the lake for 16 km through Porto Valtravaglia before reaching the important border town of Luino. The town has a long history and is well worth exploring, especially the old quarter. Garibaldi was here in 1848 leading the rebellion against Austrian occupation. Ernest Hemingway also mentions Luino and other local towns in his book *Farewell to Arms*. The town has a market on Wednesdays which is purported to be the largest in Europe! The railway station at Luino is a large and magnificent building and is completely out of proportion with the town it serves. However, the reason for this edifice was that it served as an important frontier and customs post for rail traffic to and from Switzerland. After Luino the line, having changed its electrification from the Italian 3000V DC to the Swiss 15kV AC supply, continues alongside the lake's shores through the holiday resort of Maccagno Superiore, on to Tronzano and then over the border to the small Swiss town of Ranzo-San Abbondio. The railway stays with the lake until Magadino where the Ticino river enters. The line then cuts east to the important railway junction at Bellinzona. Overall the distance from Seste Calende to Bellinzona by rail is 84 km, an enjoyable journey, and one well worth undertaking.

## I16 – Brescia to Edolo

Superb railway journeys are plentiful in this region of Italy. Another, well worth travelling is the Ferrovie Nord Milano service from the city of Brescia to Edolo, a total distance of 103 km. Brescia (population 190,000) has a long and interesting history with some commentators according its foundation to Hercules. It played an important part in resisting Fascism in World War II and received a Gold Medal in recognition. However, that was not the end of its relationship with fascism. In 1974, a bomb was left in a refuse bin near to where there was anti-fascist protest. Eight people were killed and over 90 injured. Brescia had experienced disaster before; in 1769, lightning struck the Church of San Nazaro causing a fire which ignited 90,000 kg of gunpowder which happened to be stored inside! There was a massive explosion which killed 3,000 people and destroyed one sixth of the city. After Brescia and following the line for a further 21 km to the north-west, the train arrives at Iseo. The town lies on the shores of the lesser known but nonetheless beautiful lake of Iseo, also known as Sarnico. It is the fourth largest lake in Lombardy and has a plentiful supply of fish, catches of which are served in the numerous restaurants in the many villages all round the lake. In the middle of the lake is the Monte Isola which claims to be the largest island in any lake in southern Europe. Following the line northwards, the town of Marone is reached where, 2 km north-west, at Zone, are the remarkable earth pyramids rising to over 10 m high. They were created by glacial erosion. The railway continues to run along the side of the lake. Near the top, at Pisogne, it turns north-west up the Carmonica valley following the River Oglio, the fifth longest river in Italy. The first town of any note is Darfo-Boario Terme famed for its four springs used for drinking as well as hydrotherapy. The route continues on to Breno, the chief town in the valley, and where the Parco Naturale dell'Adamello is located. The Parco dell'Adamello lies in the heart of the Rhaetian Alps and extends for 51,000 hectares (510 sq km). Mount Adamello, at 3,554 m, is the highest peak in the park. The town of Edolo (population 4,000) is the

Le NORD's Aln 668-131 drops down towards Sulzano on the shores of Lake Iseo on 28th September, 2008.

*Author*

terminus of the railway; it is a popular tourist resort, winter and summer, especially for those who enjoy walking in the mountains. To the west of Edolo are the Bergamo Alps (Pizzo Coca, 3,050 m) and to the north the Stelvio National Park running up to the border with Switzerland's Graubünden canton. Tirano is only 15 km away as the crow flies but 33 km on the twisting SS39 road. If one likes mountains, and lots of them, then Edolo is the place to go. This line is now being developed for heritage excursions using vintage diesel railcars by the Ferrovia Turistica Camuna which is part of the Ferrovie Turistiche Italiane enthusiasts' association (www.ferrovieturistiche.it) Incidentally the latter has the Treno Blu as one of its four members (*see next entry*).

## I17 – Treno Blu

A famous railway which runs from Palazzolo suil'Oglio to Paratico Sarnico on the southern tip of Lake Iseo. The railway, which is midway between Brescia and Bergamo, runs through the Parco dell'Oglio Nord. The route was closed for almost 30 years before an initiative was taken by Italian State Railways and some local municipal authorities. This led to the formation of Ferrovia del Basso Sebino (FBS) and the re-opening of the line for tourist purposes in 1994. The journey on the 11 km-long route takes 16 minutes and utilizes vintage diesel railcars on Sundays in May and June and later in September. A train journey can often be combined with an excursion by boat on the lake. Trains can also be chartered for special occasions. One of the highlights of the railway is the deployment of a 1-3-0 steam locomotive which carries the original FS number 625.177. It was built in 1922 in Berlin by Schwartzkopff who built 25 of this class out of a total of 188 constructed. Treno Blu is part of the Ferrovie Turistiche Italiane association (www.ferrovieturistiche.it) Other members of this association include the nearby Ferrovia Turistica Camuna and, in Tuscany, the Ferrovia Val d'Orcia and the Ferrovia Colle Val d'Elsa-Poggibonsi. A helpful website in Italian is www.rivadisolto.org/navigazione/trenoblu.htm

## I18 – Rittnerbahn

The Rittnerbahn (it. Ferrovia del Renon, en. Ritten Railway) originally connected Bolzano/Bozen in the Trentino-Alto Adige region with the Ritten plateau, high above the city. The metre gauge electrically-powered (now 800V DC) railway started life in 1907 as a street car operating from Walther Square to Brenner Street in the centre of the city. It shared track with the Bolzano/Bozen Tram Service which connected various local villages around Bolzano/Bozen with the city centre. From Brenner Street the line was a rack/cogwheel railway climbing 990 m to the plateau at Maria Himmelfahrt. The system operated was quite innovative. The rack locomotive was placed behind the street cars and pushed them uphill. In the middle of the climb was a siding so that trains from each direction could meet. The train, that continued down to Bolzano/Bozen, in fact produced some of the power that was necessary to take the other train up! Once on the Ritten plateau, the locomotive was uncoupled and the street cars could proceed unaided on normal tracks until reaching the final station in the village of Klobenstein. In the 1960s, a road was constructed from Bolzano/Bozen to Ritten and the popularity of the railway diminished and soon came close to being abandoned. However, it was kept open but costs had to be reduced by limiting routine maintenance. A decision was made to replace the rack/cogwheel railway with a cable car service. Shortly before the cable cars began operating, a train was derailed on the rack railway and people were killed and injured - the likely cause of the accident was thought to be due to the reduced maintenance. Today, in spite of its chequered history, the railway continues to operate all the year round but only on the Rittner plateau between Collalbo and Soprabolzano. There are hourly services each way, the journey taking 16 minutes. It is planned in 2009 that a new cable car service will be opened from Bolzano/Bozen. For more information visit the website www.ritten.com/rittnerbahn.htm

Treno Blu's Schwartzkopff-built 1-3-0 locomotive carrying FS No. 625.177 standing at Paratico Sarnico station awaiting the afternoon excursion to Palazzolo suil'Oglio on 28th September, 2008.

*Author*

Rittnerbahn tram No. 2 awaiting its passengers for the Solprabolzano-Collalbo service on 26th September, 2008. *Author*

The terminal and marshalling yards at the Brenner Pass on 10th March, 2009.                    *Author*

## I19 – Brennerbahn

A major international rail route is from Germany through Austria to Verona in Italy's Veneto region. The Brennerbahn normally refers to that section of line, 125 km in length, between Innsbruck and Bolzano/Bozen, the railway's name coming from the name of the pass (alt. 1,371 m) which the railway crosses. It is the lowest railway route across the Alps and the only one that remains in the open air, although it has to be said there are many tunnels on the way. The railway was completed in 1867 and said to have cost at that time £28 per mile! This route is always very busy transporting heavy goods vehicles (HGVs) travelling between Germany/Austria and Italy up to the Brenner Pass. The cost of an ascent or descent for an HGV on the train is about €150 (2008). Over the relatively short distance of 38 km between Innsbruck and the Brenner Pass, the altitude rises 789 m making for a steep gradient for the trains to travel, unaided by rack/cogwheel assistance. The ascent is also further hindered by serious weather problems for much of the year. In 2006 the number of trucks transported by rail on the Brenner route more than doubled, thus achieving about 70 per cent capacity use which is increasing year in year out. These issues of gradient, weather and capacity are now being addressed by the building of a new railway incorporating a Brenner Base tunnel. It is anticipated that this tunnel, between Innsbruck and Fortezza, will be 56½ km in length, making it the longest in the world. The second longest will then be the 1988-built Seikan Tunnel in Japan. The cost of the base tunnel project is estimated to be €6 billion with completion due some time between 2015 and 2020. Once operating, it is anticipated that 320 freight and 80 passenger trains will travel through the tunnel every day. This railway also features in the Austrian chapter (*see entry A24*).

## I20 – Bolzano/Bozen to Rovereto

Once passengers on trains coming from Austria have crossed the Brenner Pass and reached Bolzano/Bozen, they embark on the next stage of a most enjoyable journey to the historic and cultural city of Verona. Verona is famous, not least of all, for its operas regularly staged in its Roman amphitheatre, the third largest in Italy. Not surprisingly, Verona is included on the list of UNESCO World Heritage sites. However, the focus of this route is that which runs through the Trentino-Alto Adige's alpine ranges which terminate near to the ancient fortress town of Rovereto close to the northern end of Lake Garda. Rovereto is where 200 million-year-old Jurassic footprints were discovered in 1991 and to remind visitors of that fact as they arrive, there are three life-sized dinosaurs on display! Rovereto also claims to have the loudest sounding bell in the world. In size, it is also the largest outside Russia and East Asia. Called *Maria Dolens* (en. Grieving Virgin Mary) the bell was made between 1918 and 1925 at the inspiration of a local priest to commemorate those who had fallen in all wars. The bell still continues to be rung every day. North of Rovereto is the city of Trento, the capital of the province of the same name. The province is mainly mountainous with parts of the Dolomites within its boundaries. Important valleys are the Valle del'Adige, Val di Non, Val di Sole, Val Giudicarie and Val di Fiemme. As well as the main railway line running parallel to it is the A22 motorway. The city of Trento is famous throughout the Roman Catholic world for the 'Council of Trent' where all but three of the 25 sessions were convened between 1545 and 1563. The Council met to issue condemnations on Protestant heresies and also to define the Church's teachings on the Scripture and Tradition, Original Sin, Justification, Sacraments, the Eucharist in Holy Mass and the Veneration of Saints. The precepts of the Council of Trent stand today as re-affirmed more recently by Popes John XXIII and Paul VI. Trento is an interesting city to visit with many notable sights including the cathedral (it. duomo), fine churches and palaces as well as modernist architecture including the central post office and the railway station.

FS locomotive No. E464.034 seen here near Mezzocorona pushes a passenger service towards Bolzano/Bozen on 26th September, 2008.
*Author*

## I21 – Bolzano/Bozen to Mals (Malles)

From Bolzano/Bozen an electrified single track secondary line heads north-west alongside the River Adige and follows an 82 km journey to Mals (also referred to as Malles Venosta). The route, up the wide valley with numerous orchards and vineyards, eventually reaches the medium sized town of Merano (population 36,539). The existence of menhirs and other pre-historic findings in the area suggest there has been habitation here since the 3rd millennium BC but it was the Romans who founded the town in 15 BC. In the 13th century it became a city, later the capital of Tyrol under Austrian (Habsburg) control. After World War I, Merano became a part of Italy. Today it is a popular year-round tourist resort for Italians and Germans and in winter, there are excellent skiing opportunities. Another claim to fame for Merano was that it was here in 1981 that World Chess Championship match took place between Anatoly Karpov and Victor Korchnoi. Chess enthusiasts will know that a particular opening move was named after the town – the 'Meran Variation'. At Merano the railway heads due west first passing to the north the Parco Naturale Gruppo di Tessa and then, after Castelbello-Ciardes, the Stelvio National Park, both areas of outstanding natural beauty. The end of the line is reached at Mals (population 5,000) where 96 per cent of the inhabitants given the Austrian and Swiss influences speak German rather than Italian. The Swiss frontier at Müstair in the Graubünden canton is only 9 km away. Heading north from Mals on the SS40 highway takes the traveller up the dramatic Upper Venosta valley to San Valentino alla Muta. Here are the beautiful lakes of Resia to the north and Muta, famed for its fishing, to the south. Continuing north on the SS40, the road enters Austria's Tyrol over the Passo di Resia arriving eventually at the major Austrian town of St Anton on the Westbahn (*see entry A23*).

## I22 – Trento to Marilleva

The resort of Mezzana (alt. 1,000 m), in the heart of the Val di Sole, is accessed by train from Trento to Marilleva followed by a short drive on the SS42 highway. The setting here again is mountainous with its own Dolomites – the Brenta - not to be confused with the principal range further east. The Brenta Dolomites are the only group of mountains situated to the west of the Adige river. They extend for some 40 km and offer challenging climbing accessed by well-maintained walking routes. Their special appeal lies in the great towers of rock which, from dawn to dusk, take on a fabulous pink tone. Those interested in wildlife will find much to feed their appetite. Deer, chamois, hares and marmots, ermines, golden eagles and the mighty Alpine vulture, the lammergeyer also known as the bearded vulture, are all common. Here, it is thought, there are up to 20 brown bears still living in the wild. Trains leave Trento on a secondary single-tracked electrified line and head north running in parallel with the main line from Verona to Bolzano. At Mezzocorona, 18 km north of Trento, the line heads west following a tributary of the Adige river and then turns north again up the twisting Val di Non passing a huge lake – Lago di Santa Giustina - near to Cles before entering a long tunnel. Emerging from the tunnel near to Cagno, the route turns west and then south-west and after 10 km reaches the town of Malè, yet another popular holiday resort. The train service used to terminate here but given the popularity of Marilleva-Mezzano for winter sports the old line was re-opened in May 2003 adding seven new stations along the route, viz. Croviana, Monclassico, Dimaro-Presson, Mastellina, Mestriago, Piano and, finally, Marilleva. This Trento to Marilleva line has an interesting history. Services began in the late 1890s, but it was not officially inaugurated until October 1909. During World War I, it was used to send supplies to the troops on the front line on the Tonale. In World War II, it had a similar important role to play but at a cost. At the

A SAD-operated service utilising ATR 100 012 heads for Mals/Malles from Bolzano/Bozen seen here near Terlano on 26th September, 2008.

*Author*

Trento Provincial service near Mezzocorona on 26th September, 2008. *Author*

The Dolomites with a mid-morning FS-Trenitalia service passing through the village of Valdaora di Sotto as photographed from the main SS49 highway at Nauernhäusern on 9th March, 2009.
*Author*

end of hostilities the entire line had to be rebuilt because of damage caused by heavy bombing. The re-built line, that links Malè to Trento, is 56 km long and is a vital commuter route carrying hundreds of passengers to and from Trento every weekday. Whether or not the daily commuters appreciate the route, it is certainly one worthwhile for the traveller to experience.

### I23 – Fortezza to San Candido

Fortezza (de. Franzensfeste) 56 km north of Bolzano/Bozen and 48 km south of the Brenner Pass in the Eisacktal valley, has a small population of under 1,000. It is the departure station for what the author considers one of the 'Great Rail Journeys of Italy'. Trains depart Fortezza and pass a magnificent fortress, strategically well placed to obstruct the valley; it is now open to the public for visits in the summer. About 3 km south of Fortezza this electrified single-tracked secondary line leaves the Verona-Brenner main line and crosses the Isarco river, the second largest in the region. The line soon meets the Rienz river which it keeps in view for most of the journey to just beyond Brunico. The town has a population of 14,148 and is situated in the Val Pusteria (de. Pustertal), the northern gateway to the magnificent Dolomites. The Val Pusteria is a valley that runs east to west between Lienz in Austria's Tyrol and Mühlbach near Bressanone (de. Brixen) north of Bolzano-Bozen. The valley separates the Southern Limestone Alps from the Central Alps. Whilst the Rienz flows in the western half of the valley, the River Drava (de. Drau) flows in the east. The Dolomites are perhaps the most famous range of mountains in Italy. They are located for the most part in the province of Belluno, with other parts in the provinces of Bolzano/Bozen and Trento. Conventionally, they extend from the Adige river in the west to the Piave valley and Pieve di Cadore in the east. Incidentally, Titian was born in the late 15th century in Pieve di Cadore. The highest

mountain in the range is the Marmolada which in fact has a number of peaks, the highest of which is the Punta Penia (3,342 m). Whilst the northern border of the Dolomites is defined by the Val Pusteria, the Val Sugana defines it in the south. It is here where another attractive railway also runs (*see entry I27*). Including the Marmolada, there are a total 21 mountains over 3,000 m in height and a further 23 between 2,000 and 3,000 m. There are an amazing 36 major passes in the Dolomites, the highest on foot being the Ombretta (2,738 m) and for road traffic the Pordoi Pass (2,239 m) which connects Arabba, near Livinallongo del Col di Lana, with Canazei in the Val di Fassa. The last town in Italy before entering Austria is the popular winter and summer resort of San Candido Innichen. Here the Italian electrification of 3,000V DC ends and Austria's 15kV AC begins; whilst Italian trains do not continue on, Austrian trains do come up to San Candido. Just 8 km down the line, near Prato alla Drava, is the border. Sillian, almost 5 km further on, is the first small town encountered. This where Austria's Drautalbahn to Lienz begins (*see entry A1*).

### I24 – Pontebbana
(Tarvisio-Boscoverde to Carnia Germona del Friuli for Udine)

Trains coming from Villach in Austria via Arnoldstein operate on 15kV AC supply and can travel no further than Tarvisio-Boscoverde as the supply switches to 3000V DC. The original line here at Tarvisio was built in 1879, at that time as part of Austria's k.k. Staatsbahn; there are still traces of the original trackbed and railway architecture to be seen. However, this line was closed in 2000 with the opening of the new station and upgraded line at Tarvisio Boscoverde. Certainly, the new station is large and well appointed; it is just a pity there are not more trains! The town of Tarvisio has always been well placed commercially. For centuries, it was part of an important trade route linking the Latin, Germanic and Slavic populations of Europe. At one time, it was famous for its

The new station at Tarviso Boscoverde on 15th October, 2007 with a freight service passing through hauled with diesel assistance by locomotive No. E652.130. *Author*

'rag market' attracting shoppers from as far afield as Austria and the former Yugoslavia. Since, with the establishment of the European Community and, in particular, the 'euro zone' the market has diminished. The economy is now very much focused on winter sports following significant investment in providing skiing and related facilities. This has paid off, for example, in 2007 the Women's Alpine Skiing World Cup was held here. Travelling west from Tarvisio takes the train on the double-tracked line to the small town of Pontebba (population 1,683) which gives its name to this railway route as well as the 211 km-long highway, the SS13. During World War II, the rail line through the town was the target of heavy bombardment aimed at frustrating the German use to transport supplies to Italy. Whilst some damage was caused to the line, it was quickly repaired. The next major town down the line, which on this section is single-tracked, is Carnia. Carnia, as well as being a township, is the name of the local region which also gives its name to the Carnic Alps. It is made up of 28 municipalities (total population 39,705) located in seven beautiful valleys. Mount Coglians (2,780 m), Mount Peralba (2,694 m) and Mount Cridola (2,580 m) are the three highest mountains but there are 11 more with altitudes greater than 2,000 m. The most important river is the Tagliamento and there are many picturesque lakes, the Volaia, for example. South of Carnia the line is restored to double track working and continues down to Gemona del Friuli (population 11,167), known for its beautiful 14th century cathedral. Here, the main line continues 25 km to Udine but there is a non-electrified branch line cutting away to Sacile via Osoppo and Maniagospur. Udine, with a population of just under 100,000, is the capital of the Friuli province and like many Italian cities is well endowed with beautiful piazzas and buildings; it is well worth visiting the Piazza delle Libertà where the exquisite Loggia del Lionello can be found. It was originally constructed in the late 15th century and is now used as the town hall.

## I25 – Udine to Cividale del Friuli

From the city of Udine there is a 15 km single track non-electrified line to Cividale del Friuli, a medium-sized town close to the Slovenian border with a population of 11,547. It is situated in the foothills of the Eastern Alps and in the ravine of the picturesque Natisone river. The town was founded by Julius Caesar in 50 BC. There are many fine buildings in the town including the 15th century cathedral and the Ponte del Diavaolo (en. Devil's Bridge) spanning the river which divides the town in half. Wines are produced locally, notably the *Verduzzo friulano* (dry white) and the *Refosco dal peduncolo rosso* (classic red).

## I26 – Vittorio Veneto to Calalzo-Pieve di Cadore-Cortina

Cortina d'Ampezzo lies in the heart of the Belluno Dolomites and is a very popular tourist resort all the year round. Seeing the landscape's outstanding natural beauty, it is not difficult to see why. There used to be a railway line running to Cortina but this has long been abandoned. The trackbed has since been converted to a cycle path and more recently has been extended to Dobbiaco with the addition of a tarmac surface and lighting in the tunnels. Access now to Cortina d'Ampezzo is by train to Dobbiaco (*see entry I23*) or to Calalzo-Pieve di Cadore-Cortina and then from both towns by local bus services. The railway to Calalzo-Pieve di Cadore-Cortina is single-tracked and non-electrified from Conegliano which is on the main Venice to Udine route. From Conegliano the line passes though Vittorio Véneto to Ponte nelle Alpi. Incidentally, Vittorio Véneto was the scene of a famous 10 day battle towards the end of 1918. The Italian victory here, over the Austro-Hungarians, marked the end of World War I on the Italian front and the final achievement of Italian unification. The small town of Ponte nelle Alpi (population 8,157) is the junction with the railway from Castelfranco Veneto (*see entry I29*). The route north of Ponte nelle Alpi is very picturesque as trains head for the magnificent Dolomites. However, on the way there is a history of sadness at Longarone Zoldo. The small town (population 4,122) 12 km north of Ponte nelle Alpi, is located on the banks of the Piave. In October 1963, a landslide from Monte Toc forced 50 million cubic metres of water over the wall of the Vajont Dam, into the valley and path of the village. Tragically 1,909 people were killed by the wall of water which, it is said, was between 200 and 250 metres higher than the dam wall when it came over. At the end of the line, almost 33 km after Longarone, is the small town of Calalzo-Pieve di Cadore-Cortina which boasts a resident population of 2,415 but this is exceeded significantly by visitors throughout the year.

## I27 – Valsugana

The Valsugana is an important valley in the Trento province and hosts the single track non-electrified railway from the city of Trento to the town of Bassano del Grappa. From there the railway continues to Cittadella (for Padua) or Castelfranco Veneto (for Venice). The distance from Trento to Bassano del Grappa is 89 km. The western end of the valley near to Trento is a hugely attractive tourist area. Its popularity began as a health spa during the late 19th century when the Levico Therme baths were established access being made easier by the long established Roman-built road. The foothills of the Dolomites are to the north with a number of peaks above 2,000 m, viz. the Vigolana (2,150 m), the Monte Bondone (2,181 m) and the Paganella (2,124 m). There are two most attractive lakes to see, Lake Levico and the larger Lake Caldonazzo alongside which the railway runs for 4 km. The land in the valley is fertile as illustrated by the numerous vineyards, orchards and groves of edible horse-chestnuts. Outdoor sports are a feature of the area with climbing, hiking, mountain biking, power

A two-car unit headed by Aln 668 1238R leaves the station at Calalzo-Pieve di Cadore-Cortina towards Ponte nelle Alpi and Belluno on 27th September, 2008.

*Author*

boating, sailing, and windsurfing all on offer. Bassano del Grappa, at the end of this stretch of line is a medium-sized town with a population of 40,411; it was founded in the 2nd century BC by the Roman, Bassianus. Originally it was called Bassano Veneto but was re-named after World War I to commemorate the thousands of soldiers who lost their lives in the fierce battle on Monte Grappa (1,775 m). The Battle of Monte Grappa was fought by Italian troops against those of Austria and Germany in November and December of 1917. The fortified mountain was the last line of defence between the Austro-German armies and the Italians. Total casualties amounted to 24,000 Italians, over 4,000 British and French and in excess of 100,000 Austrian combatants. The town did not fare too well in World War II. In September 1943 the Allies signed an Armistice with Italy. This had the effect of Italy switching sides which did not go unnoticed by German troops who invaded the town and killed or deported numerous inhabitants.

FS Trenitalia service heading for Trento running alongside the Lake Caldonazzo on 25th September, 2008.

*Author*

Dueville station north of Vicenza on 20th March, 2008.

*Ivan Furlanis*

## I28 – Vicenza to Schio

The Vicenza to Schio railway runs on a single-tracked non-electrified line over a distance of 37 km. Vicenza is a city and province in the Veneto region at the foot of the Monte Berico hill where it is said the Virgin Mary appeared twice, once in March 1426 and later in August 1428. She promised that the city would be rid of the plague if a church was built on the top of a local hill. The church was built in three months! Standing there now is a beautiful basilica which has been restored repeatedly down the centuries. The basilica commands a superb view of the city, the Bacchiglione river through which it passes, and, further afield, Monte Grappa, the Dolomites, the Lessini Hills and the Venetian lagoon. Continuing from Vicenza the town of Dueville (population 13,988) is reached and after a little further the townships of Marano Vicentino and Thiene before arriving at Schio, a medium-sized town (population 39,000). The town is surrounded by the the Italian Prealps (Little Dolomites) and specifically Mount Pasubio. By the 12th century, Schio had become prosperous as an important centre of the wool industry. In the 19th century the local wool industry expanded, in particular with the investment by Alessandro Rossi who founded the company *Lanerossi*. Along with other companies – Conte and Cazzola – the town became known as the 'Manchester of Italy' both connurbations owing their success to the wool trade. Rossi was a generous benefactor to the town; he built houses, nurseries, schools, theatres and parks for his workers. The 'Weaver's Monument' stands in the town, unveiled in 1879 by Alessandro Rossi and dedicated to his workers. The statue represents a man holding proudly in one hand the shuttle of his loom, the emblem of his craft and the industry. And, by the way, what happened to Vicenza's plague? It did not continue!

## I29 – Castelfranco Veneto to Belluno

The railway, single track and non-electrified, from Castelfranco Veneto passes through Montebelluna (famous for its modern art festivals) and Feltre, before reaching Belluno, a distance of 84 km. The town of Belluno (population 36,042) is the main terminus of services on the line. From here a service runs to Ponte nelle Alpi and on to Calalzo-Pieve di Cadore-Cortina (*see entry I25*). Trains coming up from Conegliano divert temporarily at Ponte nelle Alpi to Belluno before returning to Ponte nelle Alpi and continuing up the valley to Calalzo-Pieve di Cadore-Cortina. Judging by the size of the station and the now little-used marshalling yards, the station has been an important railway location in its time. Belluno is the largest community in the area and one of the 15 municipalities in the national park of the Belluno Dolomites. To the north of the town is the imposing Schiara range with Gusela del Vescova and Mounts Serva and Talvena forming the backdrop. To the south is the Nevegal resort in the Castionese area, well known for its skiing. Belluno derives its name from the celtic *belo-dunum* which means 'splendid hill' and looking at the local scenery, it is certainly a most apt description. The Romans founded the town about 200 BC and given its strategic location it became an important military stronghold in Roman Venetia. After the fall of the Roman Empire it was successively ruled by the Lombards, the Carolingians and some powerful families before giving itself to the Republic of Venice in 1404. Thereafter the town became an important hub for the transport of wood from Cadore down the Piave river. Notable sights in the town include several churches and a beautiful late 15th century cathedral. The church of Santo Stefano is of particular note in housing several 15th century paintings by local masters and including an *Adoration of the Magi* from Tiziano's workshop . Tiziano, better known as Titian, was born not far away in Pieve di Cadore.

Belluno station on 27th September, 2008 with, *on the left*, Aln 668 1238R awaiting departure for Calalzo-Pieve di Cadore-Cortina, and, *on the righ*t, a train powered by D445.1098 about to depart for Montebelluna via Feltre.

*Author*

# Slovenia and Croatia

## Introduction

Continuing our journey eastwards through the Alps from Italy brings the traveller to Slovenia (*Republika Slovenija*) the most northerly country in what was formerly part of Yugoslavia until it gained its independence in 1991. The capital city is Ljubljana which, with over 270,000 inhabitants, is its largest conurbation. The overall population of Slovenia was estimated in 2009 to be 2,053,355.

Slovenia's neighbours are Italy to the west, Austria to the north, Hungary to the north-east and Croatia to the south, another former Yugoslavian province.

Four distinct geographical regions converge in Slovenia, i.e. the Alps, the Dinarides or Dinaric Alps, the large central Pannonian Plain, and the Mediterranean (Adriatic Sea). The main alpine ranges in Slovenia are in the Eastern Alps, i.e the Julian Alps, Kamnik Alps (sometimes referred to as the Savinja Alps) and the Pohorje, a lower range of mountains. These ranges all run south of the Austrian border which is delineated by the Karawanken Alps. The highest summit in Slovenia, located to the west of Jesenice in the Julian Alps, is the Triglav (2,864 m) which literally means 'three headed' named after its distinctive three-peaked outline.

The Slovenian Alps are accessed from Italy via six road crossings, i.e. from Tarvisio to Ratece, a very minor road crossing near Zaga in Slovenia; another over the Passo di Predil; from Cividale to Robic; and two roads near to Nova Gorica. Austria's road access to Slovenia is through the Loibl pass and tunnel (length 1.57 km); and from Klagenfurt to Kranj. However, to the east the prime route since 1991 is a toll road through the Karawanken Motorway Tunnel (length 7.86 km). This provides the fastest link between Villach and Klagenfurt to Ljubljana. Moving east from Jesenice there is a high road (1,280 m) into Austria at Jezerski (Seebergsattel); at Lavamünd there is a route to Dravograd; and, finally a major road and motoway crossing from Graz to Maribor.

There are three railway routes in the Alps into Slovenia from Austria and three from Italy. The principal international route into Slovenia from Austria is at Rosenbach and through the Karawanken railway tunnel to Jesenice. A second crossing is from Spielfeld-Straß, near Graz to Maribor and another from Bleiburg to Holmec, near Dravograd. There was a fourth route from Lavamünd to Dravograd but the line has since been closed.

From Italy there are three freight/industrial workings around Nova Gorica, Villa Opicina and Sezana. Special steam trains, however, do operate fortnightly in summer between Gorizia in Italy and Bled near Jesenice.

That part of northern Yugoslavia which is now called Slovenia had its first railways in 1841 when the then Austrian Empire began construction of the Südliche Staatsbahn (Austrian Southern Railway) between Vienna and the major commercial port of Trieste, now in Italy. This allowed for Maribor to have a rail connection to Graz in 1844. Two years later it was extended via Pragersko to Celje and then on through, what has now become an important railway junction, Zidani Most, eventually reaching Ljubljana in 1849. A double-tracked line was continued via Postojna, Pivka and Diva a arriving at Trieste in 1857. In the early part of the 20th century, numerous other railways were built. In 1860, Pragersko was connected to Ormož and further to  akovec in Croatia. In 1862, a railway was built along the Sava river connecting Zidani Most with what is now Croatia's capital, Zagreb. In 1863, the Carinthian Railway was built following the route of the Drava

SŽ service No. 312-123 leaves Jesenice for Ljubljana on 16th October, 2007.

*Author*

river, thus connecting Maribor with Dravograd, Klagenfurt and Villach. Seven years later, Ljubljana had a rail connection with Kranj, Jesenice and Tarvisio in Italy. In 1873, a line from Pivka via the town of Ilirska Bistrica connected with the important port of Rijeka. Between 1904 and 1906, the Bohinj Railway, also known as the Transalpina Railway, was built (*see entries SLO 2 & SLO3*).

Today, Slovenske Železnice (SŽ) is Slovenia's state railway which was founded in 1991 born out of the Ljubljana Division of the former Yugoslavia Railways, the Jugoslovenske Železnice (JŽ). Slovenian Railways operates 1,229 km of standard gauge tracks, 331 km of which are double-tracked. There are good connections with surrounding countries as a result of the earlier influence of the Austro-Hungarian Empire. Just over 500 km of Slovenia's network is electrified to the Italian standard of 3000V DC. However, the remainder of the former lines that have been electrified operate on a 25kV AC supply.

**Croatian Railways** (Hrvatske Željeznice - HŽ) the Croatian railway network comprises 2,974 km of track, of which 248 km is double track. Just over 40 per cent is electrified. Of great importance to Croatia and of closest relevance to the Alpine theme of this book are the major routes from Ljubljana via Dobova to Zagreb and on to Tovarnik on the border with Serbia; Ljubliana to Rijeka via Logatec, Pivka and Ilirska Bistrica; and, Rijeka to Zagreb via Delnice, Ogulin/Oštanje and Karlovac.

The Dinaric Alps are to the south of Ljubljana and are separated from the main Alpine ranges by a large plain. The whole range of these Alps down into Serbia/Montenegro do not qualify for entry in this book but given the close proximity of two routes, brief mention is given to them.

## The Railways

### SLO1 – Jesenice to Kranj

Jesenice (de. Aßling) is a medium-sized town on the Slovenian side of the Karavanken mountain range, longest of all the Alpine ranges and which forms the border with Austria to the north. It is the home of Slovenia's largest steel company, Acroni. The history of Jesenice is closely related to its iron industry which has been the principal driver for the town's development. Incidentally, the town's name derives from the Slovenian word *jêsen* meaning ash tree, of which many flourished here at one time. Jesenice, being a border town, has international importance for rail communications. Trains, mainly freight of Austrian origin, arrive and leave the vast rail terminal benefiting from the Karawanken rail tunnel (length 7,976 m) opened in 1906 by Archduke Franz Ferdinand, later assassinated in Sarajevo. Kranj, situated on the banks of the Sava river, is the fourth largest city (population 53,000) in Slovenia and centre of the Upper Carniola region. It is mainly an industrial city with significant electronics and rubber industries. It is 35 km from Jesenice and 20 km from Ljubljana. Ljubljana's international airport is nearby. Kranj has an interesting medieval centre, a 14th century church (dedicated to St Cantianus) and a mid-16th century fortification, the Khislstein Castle. Concerts are occasionally held there in the grounds.

### SLO2 – Bohinj Railway

Lying to the west of Jesenice is the Trigalvski Narodni Park. It is Slovenia's only national park named after Triglav, which is the highest mountain in the park and in Slovenia (2,864 m). The

Jesenice station, departure point for trains to Ljubljana and Nova Gorica on 9th July, 2007. In view are SŽ railcar No. 312-134 and locomotive No. 363-026.

*Author*

mountain is an important national symbol and is featured on the national coat of arms as well as the country's flag. The Triglav National Park, one of the earliest of Europe's parks, was founded in 1924 and extends along the Italian border and close to the Austrian border. Its territory is almost identical with that defined by the Eastern Julian Alps. The park covers 880 sq. km, about three per cent of Slovenia's total area. The Bohinj rail route from Jesenice to Nova Gorica is sometimes called the Transalpina Railway and also the Wocheinerbahn. It is approximately 72 kilometres long, single-tracked and not electrified. It follows the south-eastern boundary of the national park for about 50 km of the journey. On leaving Jesenice trains run south-west to Bled, well known for its lake which is a major tourist attraction. Perched on a rock overlooking the lake is the medieval Bled Castle. The lake is also renowned for its calm waters providing ideal conditions for rowers. It hosted the World Rowing Championships in 1966, 1979, and 1989 and will do so again in 2011. There is an island on the lake which houses the Church of the Assumption of Mary Pilgrimage, ascent to which is by way of 99 steps. Weddings take place at this church from time to time and tradition has it that the groom must carry his bride up these steps, during which time she must remain silent; the author makes no comment! Moving on from Bled's Jazero station, the train continues to Bohinjska Bistrica (population 1,891) a large village and popular tourist resort with numerous hotels and restaurants. The village is the home of the Tomaža Godca museum focusing on the World War I battles which were fought in the local mountains on the Isonzo (aka Soča) between 1915 and 1917. Total casualties arising out of the numerous battles were enormous. Half of the entire Italian World War I casualties, some 300,000, were suffered along the

Isonzo. Austro-Hungarian losses, whilst not as numerous were, nonetheless, extremely high at around 200,000. Next stops on the route are Kneza, Baca, Kanal ob Soči (an important crossing point of the river) and finally Deskle, the last station before reaching Nova Gorica, a relatively young city (population 32,000) built after World War II. Nova Gorica came about after the 1946 Paris Peace Conference which had decided that the county of Primorska (east of Trieste) be ceded to that part of Yugoslavia, now Slovenia, but the city of Gorizia was to remain in Italy; 'New Gorizia' was the planned response. This route benefits from steam-hauled excursions in the summer (*see next entry*).

### SLO3 – Nova Gorica Bled Steam Excursions

During the summer each year, special excursions depart from the railway station of Gorizia in Italy calling at Nova Gorica and Most na Soči in Slovenia bound for Bled, near Jesenice. The route taken is on the historical Transalpina Railway which was inaugurated on 19th July, 1906. The construction of the railway was in those times very complicated and presented plenty of challenges in the building of numerous tunnels, bridges and viaducts etc. Especially remarkable is the Solkan bridge with its 85 m-long arch, which is still world's largest, and the Podbrdo tunnel, also known as the Bohinj tunnel (6,339 m), passing under Mount Kobla (1,498 m) in the Julian Alps. The train, travelling along the beautiful valleys of the Soča (it. Isonzo) and the Sava, is usually hauled by a steam locomotive from the Railway Museum (Železniska Muzej) in Ljubljana. However, after prolonged periods without rain, and if there is a serious threat of fire, a diesel locomotive has to substitute. On arrival at Bled

Steam locomotive No. 33-037 hauling a Club excursion towards Nova Gorica on 5th May, 2007.

*Leon Hmeljak*

station a bus transfers passengers to the castle for a guided tour followed by lunch in a restaurant above the lake. After lunch there is some free time for visiting the town and the lake. Later passengers are transferred back to the station for the return journey to Nova Gorica; all in all a splendid day out. For more information, visit the website also written in English, Italian and German www.club.si The railway museum in Ljubljana retains 53 standard gauge locomotives, four of which are in operational service and nine narrow gauge locomotives, one of which is active. Helpful websites to visit for more detail are: www.slo-zeleznice.si/en/about_us/railway_museum and for listings see www.burger.si/MuzejiInGalerije/ZelezniskiMuzej/SeznamLokomotiv2.html

## SLO4 – Dravograd to Maribor

Dravograd (de. Unterdrauburg) is a small town (population 8,863) located on the Slovenian-Austrian border where the Drava River meets the Meža and Mislinja rivers. Maribor (de. Marburg an der Drau) is the second largest city in Slovenia with a population of approximately 133,000. Maribor also lies on the banks of the River Drava near to the Pohorje mountain range, the principal peaks being the Rogla (1,517 m), rni Vrh (1,533 m), Velika Kopa (1,542 m) and Veliki Vrh (1,347 m). From Klagenfurt a standard gauge railway used to run to Dravograd via Grafenstein, Bleiburg (last station in Austria) and Holmec. At present it is understood that Slovenian diesel railcars only run to Bleiburg from Holmec. The Lavamünd route from Austria to Dravograd is closed. To the east Slovenian trains run one service per day from Maribor via Šentilj to Graz via Spielfeld-Straß. From Dravograd the railway, opened in 1863, ran for about 50 km to Maribor, 60 km south of Graz. Judging

Former JŽ 1927-built Kraus-Linz locomotive No. 18-005 seen here at Dravograd station on 16th October, 2007. In its time this locomotive was capable of 90 kmh but not nowadays!    *Author*

by the deserted station and marshalling yards at Dravograd not a lot happens there nowadays. Latest information suggests that a few trains – five per day - travel between Maribor and Dravograd. For more information visit the official website www.slo-zeleznice.si which helpfully is in English.

## SLO5 – Ljubljana to Kamnik-Graben

Kamnik is a small town with a population of 26,618. The area nearby is a large part of the Kamnik Alps. The name Kamnik was first mentioned in the 11th century and as a town in 1229 when it was an important trading post on the road between Ljubljana and Cole. The town is one of the oldest in Slovenia. In

SŽ service to Kamnik-Graben seen near Domzale, north of Ljubljana, on 16th October, 2007 operated by railcar No. 814/813-041. *Author*

## SLO6 – Logatec to Ilirska Bistrica

Logatec (population 11,343) is a small town located in the Inner Carniola region between Ljubljana and Postojna. The area is mostly covered by forests and is popular for biking and hiking routes. The town of Ilirska Bistrica (population 1,423) is a major economic centre of the district. It is the last town in Slovenia before entering Croatia. Like Logatec, the town is popular with tourists, especially hikers wishing to climb to the peak of Mount Snežnik (1,796 m). The town is also well known for its brass orchestra founded in 1913. The railway route arrives here from Ljubljana via Postojna and Pivla. It is a main line double-tracked and electrified to the 3000V DC standard and continues so over the border to Šapjane (*see next entry*).

Two Croatian Railways (HŽ) electric Bo-Bo locomotives Nos. 1141 209 and 1141 229 photographed at Zagreb station in 2002. *Author*

the Middle Ages it even had its own Mint. The town was among the most influential centres of power for the Bavarian Counts of Andechs Carniola region at the time. The only remaining evidence of their residency are the two ruined castles built on high ground near to the town centre. There is a Franciscan Monastery in the town which is well preserved having undergone extensive renovation in recent years. Also of interest is Zaprice Castle, which stands outside the town and was built in a later period. Most of the old town is built in the Austro-Hungarian style with many of the facades renovated in recent years. There are 15 services per day between Kamnik-Graben and Ljubljana's Šiška station.

## HR 1 – Ilirska Bistrica to Delnice

On leaving Slovenia the first station in Croatia is Šapjane, a typical border rail town. Here, the route to Jurdani, Rijeka and Delnice remains electrified but becomes single track. From Jurdani the railway heads east to Rijeka, the principal seaport of Croatia, located on Kvarner Bay, at the head of the Adriatic Sea. It is Croatia's third largest city and has a population of 144,043 inhabitants which almost doubles when the greater conurbation is taken into account. The majority of its citizens, four out of five, are Croats. Rijeka, incidentally, means 'river' in Croatian. The city's economy is largely dependent on sea transport, shipbuilding and tourism. One claim to fame is that it was in Rijeka that the self-propelled torpedo (*tvornica*) was invented by Giovanni Luppis in the mid-1860s. The remains of his factory still exist, including a well-preserved launch ramp used for testing the first torpedo in 1866. Further east is Delnice, now a tourist centre, and which is the largest settlement (population 4,451) in the mountainous region of Gorski Kotar. The highest mountains there are the Bjelolasica (1,534 m) and the Risnjak (1,528 m), the latter giving its name to the local national park.

Former Yugoslavian locomotive plinthed near to Zagreb station photographed in 2002.

*Author*

# Austria

## Introduction

Northwards from Slovenia lies the Republic of Austria, a landlocked country in central Europe with a population of 8.3 million. To the north are the countries of Germany and the Czech Republic, to the east are Slovakia and Hungary, to the south Slovenia and Italy and Switzerland and Liechtenstein lie to the west. The capital and also a state in its own right is the city of Vienna (population 1,680,266) which lies on the banks of the River Danube. The other states from east to west are Burgenland, Lower Austria, Styria, Carinthia, Upper Austria, Salzburg, Tyrol and Vorarlberg. All but four - Vienna, Burgenland, Lower Austria and Upper Austria - enjoy alpine status.

**Tyrol** (Tirol) is perhaps the best-known alpine state. It is in fact in two parts separated by a 20 km strip of land by the Salzburg state. The two halves are identified as North Tyrol and East Tyrol. The capital is Innsbruck (population 118,000) which, after Grenoble in France, is also the second largest city in the Alps. Innsbruck is known for its university and for modern techniques in medicine especially treating skiing injuries! Tyrol, of course, is popular for its famous skiing resorts, such as Kitzbühel, Ischgl and St Anton. Other important towns in the Tyrol are Kufstein, Schwaz, Reutte and Landeck.

**Styria** is in south-eastern Austria and adjoins Slovenia, the latter is sometimes known locally as Lower Styria. It is the southern part of the state that is closest to the alpine mountains. The capital city is Graz in the east.

**Carinthia** (Kärnten) extends over the Carnic Alps and the Karawanken Alps which together form a natural border with the Friuli-Venezia-Giulia province in Italy and with the Republic of Slovenia. The Hohe Tauern mountain range separates Carinthia to the north from the state of Salzburg. The capital is Klagenfurt with Villach being the second most important city and an important railway junction.The main river is the Drau also known as the Drava.

**Salzburg** is a small state in population (530,000) of which almost one quarter live in the capital city of Salzburg. In the south of the state are the main ranges of the Central Alps including part of the Hohe Tauern mountains with numerous peaks over 3,000 m.

**Vorarlberg** (population 373,000) is to the west and is the wealthiest state in Austria, albeit the smallest in area after Vienna. The capital is Bregenz although the largest city is the industrial centre Dornbirn which is almost three times its size. The notable mountain ranges in Vorarlberg are the Eastern Alps of the Silvretta, the Rätikon, the Verwall and the Arlberg. The state again is famous for its winter sports, there being many famous skiing resorts such as Lech, Zürs, Schruns, Warth, Damüls and Brand. Damüls also happens to have the worldwide record for being the town with most annual snowfall, average 9.30 metres. The highest mountain in the state is Piz Buin (3,312 m).

As can be gathered already from the description of the states, Austria is a mountainous country with over 60 per cent of its territory being in the Eastern Alps. This main collection is made up of the Lavanttal Alps, Niedere Tauern, the Nock Mountains, the Hohe Tauern, Kitzbühel Alps and the Zillertal Alps. The highest peak in the Austria is the Gross Glockner (3,797 m) which is located in the Carinthia's Hohe Tauern range, north of Lienz.

Road access to Austria's Alps can be achieved from Switzerland through Feldkirch on a road and motorway running through St Anton to Innsbruck.

From Italy, the routes are the St Valentino alla Muta to Landeck via the Passo di Rosia; the Merano to Sölden route via the Passo del Rombo; the Brenner (Brennero) Pass taking traffic from Bolzano/Bozen to Innsbruck; and, finally, from Dobbiaco-Toblach in the Dolomites to Lienz.

Access from Slovenia is from Kranj to Klagenfurt over the Loibl pass and/or tunnel (length 1,570 m). In the east, the Karawanken Motorway Tunnel (length 7,864 m) provides a fast link between Ljubljana and Villach and Klagenfurt. In the east there is a high road (1,280 m) into Austria at Jezerski (Seebergsattel); from Lavamünd there is a route to Dravograd; and, finally, a major road and motorway crossing from Maribor to Graz.

Roads from the German Alps into Austria, from west to east, are between Sondhofen and Weißenbach via the Oberjoch Pass; roads from Nasselwand and Füssen meet at the border *en route* to Reutte; and, there is a high mountain road from Oberammergau also travelling to Reutte. There are two routes from Garmisch-Partenkirchen, one to Imst and the other to Innsbruck. A major road and a motorway links Innsbruck with the Munich-Salzburg motorway via Kufstein. There are three crossings east of Kufstein, i.e. from Aschau to Walchsee; Schleching and Reit im Winkl both heading for Kössen; and, Bad Reichenhall for Lofer via the Steinpaß.

There are 10 railway connections into the Austrian Alps from Switzerland/Liechtenstein (FL), Italy, Slovenia and Germany.

From Switzerland via Liechtenstein there is just one route which arrives at Feldkirch from Buchs via Schaan-Vaduz (Liechtenstein) or direct from St Margrethen. From Italy there are three railway routes – the important Brenner crossing; a second from San Candido to Sillian for Lienz; and, finally, the Pontebbana route which runs from Tarvisio-Boscoverde to Arnoldstein.

There is only one main international railway route from Slovenia into Austria, i.e. to Villach and Klagenfurt through the Karawanken railway tunnel from Jesenice.

The connections with Germany are made through Feldkirch (for the Arlbergbahn); from Lindau via Bregenz and Dornbirn; from Kempten to Pfronten-St Steinach (Germany-Austrian border); from Reutte to Griesen (Austrian-German border); and, from Garmisch-Partenkirchen to Innsbruck via Mittenwald. The only other route into Austria and a major one at that is via Kufstein connecting Rosenheim from Munich with Worgl for Innsbruck.

## The Railways

### A1 – Drautalbahn

The River Drau is a major tributary of the River Danube. It rises near Dobbiaco Toblach in the Carnic Alps in Italy and flows eastward through Austria's Tyrol (east) and Carinthia states in what is the longest longtitudinal valley in the Alps, the Drautal, and from which this railway derives its name. After leaving Austria it flows south-eastwards into Slovenia, where it becomes known as the Drava, and on in to Croatia where it joins the Mur (Mura) river eventually forming part of the Croatian/Hungarian border. The railway runs from San Candido in Italy (*see entry I23*) near the Austrian border via Weitlanbrunn to Lendorf where it joins the Tauernbahn (*see entry A14*), a total distance of almost 207 km. The route is single track all the way and electrified to the Austrian standard of 15kV AC. Whilst the railway enters from San Candido Innichen in Italy, most services operate from the first serious large village over the border, Sillian (population 2,097). A claim to fame for Sillian is that Richard Strauss (1864-1949) stayed at the local Schwarzer Adler hotel where he is purported to have played the hotel piano and perhaps to have composed there as well. A less prestigious claim is the ancient pillary in the village square which was used mostly to punish adulterous women. As the train travels from Sillian to the medieval town of Lienz (population 12,125) a magnificent series of mountains form a corridor on either side. For example, to the north in the Hohe Tauern range is the Thurntaler (2,408 m), Kühegg (2,253 m), Finsterkofel (2,633 m), the Böses Weibele (2,521 m) and, of course, Austria's highest mountain, the Gross Glockner (3,797 m). To the south are the Lienzer Dolomiten which forms the frontier with Italy including the Helm (2,433 m), Hochegg (2,477 m), Golzentipp (2,317 m) and the Spitzkofel (2,717 m). Beyond Lienz the corridor is equally attractive as it passes the Kreuzeck group of mountains to the north keeping tight hold of the

'Taurus' class 1216 No. 013-3 hauls an ÖBB passenger service from Sillian towards Lienz on 9th March, 2009. *Author*

River Drau as it flows east. There is little doubt that the route of this river offers something special for the visitor to enjoy. For that reason, it is not surprising to learn that the Drau cycle path has been developed and runs for 366 km from its source through Austria's East Tyrol and Carinthia to Maribor in Slovenia. In the medium term, it is hoped to extend the path all the way to the Black Sea.

## A2 – Gailtalbahn

The railway from Arnoldstein to Kötschach-Mauthen is known as the Gailtalbahn taking its name from the River Gail which it follows for almost the entire 62 km journey. The river is 122 km in length and eventually drains into the River Drau near Villach. The valley

A Gailtalbahn service operated by double railcar No. 5047 041-8 near Nötsch on 18th October, 2007.                      *Author*

through which the river flows attract several species of rare birds making it an important location for ornithologists. The railway was the initiative of an industrialist Arnold Steiner Felix von Mottony who was granted the concession to build it in 1893. The first section, 30.7 km in length, from Arnoldstein to Hermagor was opened to traffic in August 1894. Hermagor is a small town (population *circa* 20,000) and a popular tourist location, especially for winter sports at Nassfeld. Nassfeld-Hermagor boasts over 110 km of pistes and is considered to be one of Austria's 'Top 10' skiing areas. The second section of the railway to Kötschach-Mauthen followed during World War I, built mostly by prisoners of war. The railway was damaged during the war but was fully restored by mid-1918. Kötschach-Mauthen, 34 km west of Hermagor, is a large village (population 3,539) and is a well-known spa and 'wellness' centre. It is the railway's terminus. Kötschach-Mauthen is the gateway to the Lesachtal valley, a beautiful area of Austria sandwiched between the Lienzer Dolomites and the Gailtal Alps. The full journey on the non-electrified route takes 86 minutes. The largest structure on the Gailtalbahn is 60 m-long bridge over the River Gail located 3 km north of Arnoldstein.

## A3 – Die Reißeck-Höhenbahn

Near to the village of Kolbnitz (alt. 747 m) 67 km north-west of Villach, is a combined funicular and mountain railway. The Reißeck group of mountains is the destination with the Reißeck mountain itself being the highest point at 2,965 m above sea level. The journey begins on the funicular, 3,576 m in length. It was constructed in three stages after World War II. The first section was to Schütters and completed in March 1950, to Trog by June 1953 and finally reaching Schoberboden (alt. 2,237 m) in March 1954. The railway line to which the funicular connects was built in 1948 specifically to transport materials for the construction of a hydroelectric scheme in the mountains. In 1953 the railway line was opened to tourists. Operating at an altitude greater than 2,200 m, this is the highest privately-owned railway in Austria. It has a narrow gauge of 600 mm. Today, the railway not only transports tourists but also continues to transport maintenance staff to the hydroelectric power stations. The journey takes 25 minutes on the funicular, climbing at angles varying between 25 and 82 per cent before arriving at the Schoberboden terminal. The railway then takes 10 minutes for the journey from Schoberboden to the Reißeck mountain restaurant. The distance covered is almost 3.4 km, of which a third is through the Reißeck Tunnel. The gradient on the railway never exceeds 3.9 per cent. On arrival at the restaurant the rest of any journey is taken on foot. From the restaurant there are a number of mountain hikes of varying degrees of difficulty. A very popular short walk takes the visitor to the Mühldorf reservoir.

Hohenbahn's Reißeck funicular awaiting departure on 18th October, 2007. *Author*

There are plenty of information points on the route providing helpful explanations about the countryside, its geology and vegetation. A particularly interesting point is the 'echo spot' near to the reservoir. The Reißeck-Höhenbahn is open daily from mid-May to mid October but it pays to check beforehand. It has been known to be closed by snow in July! For more information, see the website www.tauerntouristik.at/en/reisseck/

### A4 – Karawankenbahn

The Karawanken Alps, at 120 km, is the longest mountain range in Europe and a natural boundary between Austria and Slovenia. The Karawankenbahn is the prime international connection between the two countries connecting the Austrian cities of Villach and Klagenfurt on the northern side and Jesenice in Slovenia in the south. Villach (population 58,480) is the second largest city in Carinthia and is an important railway hub in southern Austria. As well as mountains as neighbours, Villach has several large lakes nearby, including Lake Ossiach, Lake Faak, Silbersee, Vassacher See, Magdalensee and St Leonharder See. As a consequence it is very popular with tourists. Villach also has an unusually long-running carnival each year – it starts on 11th November and concludes on 4th March! Klagenfurt (population 92,404) situated on Lake Worthensee, is the capital of Carinthia and the sixth largest city in Austria. The city has a long and interesting history as is reflected in the many attractive buildings and monuments which have survived, in spite of heavy bombing in World War II. Jesenice, with a population of 21,620, is much smaller than its two neighbours. It owes much of its existence to the iron and metallurgy industries. The railway connection between Austria and Slovenia was inaugurated in the autumn of 1906 with the completion of the rail tunnel under the Karawanken mountains. It was opened by Archduke Franz Ferdinand. The tunnel is 7.976 km-

Rosenbach station with diesel locomotive No. 2016 043-8 having brought a passenger service from Villach on 15th October, 2007.

*Caroline Jones*

NBiK's Gmeinder diesel No. 2061.201 and other rolling stock at the Weizeldorf station and depot on 9th July, 2007.                 *Author*

long making it the fourth longest in Austria and the longest in Slovenia. The rail tunnel is 112 m longer than the neighbouring road tunnel completed in 1991. The main railway route to Jesenice is from Villach and not Klagenfurt. Trains leave Villach main station and travel 5.4 km south to Gödersdorf near to which there is a huge freight marshalling centre. At this point on the route the line, whilst still electrified, reduces to single track. The railway then runs eastwards along the foot of the mountains until it reaches Rosenbach, a small village at the foot of the Reißmannkogel (alt. 1,724 m) where the route is restored to double track working. The main railway continues as double track for the 2 km down to the mouth of the tunnel into which it disappears emerging a little later close to Jesenice. The length of the route between Villach and Jesenice is 38 km and the journey takes 37 minutes.

## A5 – Nostalgiebahn in Kärnten (NBiK)

The route from Klagenfurt to Rosenbach is 34.6 km long and is known as the Rosentalbahn. It is a single track non-electrified line but nowadays there is little passenger traffic on the route as most of the local needs are fulfilled by bus services. For this reason, the Rosentalbahn does not qualify for a full entry. Twelve kilometres down the route from Klagenfurt is the village of Weizelsdorf. Here is located Nostalgiebahn in Kärnten, an enthusiasts' railway which runs on its own exclusive standard gauge track from Weizelsdorf to Ferlach. The line, which was part of the ÖBB network until 1951, measures 5.7 km in length. Ferlach (population 7,404) claims to be the southernmost town in Austria. There is a 'Museum für Technik und Verkehr Historama' located at Ferlach which is run by the railway enthusiasts. There is also a shop and restaurant. The railway preserves two steam locomotives, both built in Austria at Lokomotivf. Vienna Florisdorf, one in 1927 and the other in 1941. There are also a number of diesel locomotives and an interesting

collection of restored/preserved carriages. The railway operates at weekends from early July to early September each year and from time to time runs excursions out on the main line east as far as Faak am See, a distance of 20 km from Weizelsdorf. More information can be found at the website www.nostalgiebahn.at

## A6 – Höllentalbahn

The railway, also known as Museumsbahn Payerbach-Hirschwang, through the 'Hell Valley' as it is sometimes referred to, traces its origins back to the beginning of the 20th century. At that time there was a perceived need for a rail connection from the Semmeringbahn at Payerbach to the small industrial village of Hirschwang. The engineering company charged with building this 5 km standard gauge line decided first to develop a 'construction railway'. A railway line was built using the 'Bosnian' 760 mm gauge for transporting materials. The traction used to haul the building materials was steam-powered locomotives, built in 1903 and which had previously been used for the construction of the Karawanken tunnel (*see entry A4*). Construction was not helped by many delays and later by the onset of war. At the end of World War I, it was decided to abandon the standard gauge project and its intended tunnel. The construction railway, however, was kept going and used to support industry in Hirschwang. In 1926, the narrow gauge railway was reinforced and extended and new 'ultra-modern' four-axle railcars with trailers were purchased. This was the start of the Lokalbahn Payerbach-Hirschwang (LBP-H) which over the following 37 years transported millions of industry workers as well as tourists. In 1963, the railway was abandoned in favour of bus services. Fortunately, 14 years later, the Österreichische Gesellschaft für Lokalbahnen, ÖGLB, for short (en. Austrian Light Rail Association) was founded and established a museum railway service operating with freight trains until the early 1980s. The

Tram No. 1 leaves Reichenau heading for Hirschwang on 14th October, 2007.
*Caroline Jones*

electricity supply, incidentally, is 550V DC delivered by catenaries with energy coming from rotating and static AC-DC transformers. Today, the railway continues to operate using diesel and electric locomotives maintained by a small group of volunteers. This limits services to Sundays and public holidays in the summer. Nonetheless, the Höllentalbahn is a delight to thousands of visitors every year and is well worth visiting. For more information, visit the website www.lokalbahnen.at/hoellentalbahn/info.html

### A7 – Mariazellerbahn

The Mariazellerbahn, sometimes referred to as 'The Pilgrim's Railway', runs from St Pölten to Mariazell, a total distance of 85 km. The journey takes up to 2½ hours. Ideas of building this railway go back to the mid-19th century but it did not become a reality until 1898 when the first section from St. Pölten to Kirchberg was opened. Owing to the challenging nature of the terrain with many tight curves to negotiate, it was decided that a narrow 760 mm gauge should be used. The first trains that ran on this route were hauled by steam locomotives, one of which, is on static display at St Pölten station. Extending the railway to Mariazell took some time; indeed, it was a full eight years before the first freight train arrived there and six months later the first passenger train. The railway enjoyed immediate success encouraging the owners to expand. Using steam-hauled services alone could not cope with demand so a decision was made to adopt electrification, then in its infancy. There being no precedents it was agreed to install 6,500V AC making it the first main line to be electrified. By 1911, tests had shown the viability of the system and operations began in earnest. The railway is today still using much of the original equipment installed by Siemens almost a hundred years ago, saying much about the quality of the craftsmanship of the time. The railway enjoyed continuing success for many decades but in the 1990s freight traffic came to an end. The increasing popularity of the

Mariazellerbahn's *nostalgie* train hauled by electric locomotive No. 1099.02 from St Pölten near Laubenbachmühle on 7th October, 2007.
*Caroline Jones*

motor car also led to declining numbers of passengers putting the line under threat of closure. Fortunately, the struggle to survive was championed by rail enthusiasts who managed to re-awaken the interest of the general public. This was partly helped by the re-introduction of steam-hauled services after some railway employees purchased and restored an original steam engine and returned it to working the line. This initiative met with immediate success and it became quite clear that there was future for the line. The 'Verein Freunde der Mariazellerbahn' was founded with the objective of restoring regular train services. Matters have since improved with NÖVOG, the regional organization responsible for

local transport, being active in keeping the Mariazellerbahn operational. The recent introduction of the Panoramic 760 service was hoped to re-generate more interest in the line but this has not achieved all it set out to do. Nonetheless, the continuing running of steam has been welcomed, as evidenced by the ever-growing numbers of passengers. The Mariazell Museum Tramway, located at Mariazell, is linked to this railway. For more information, visit www.mariazellerbahn.at/en and/or www.noevog.at

### A8 – Schneebergbahn

At 2,076 metres above sea level, the Schneeberg is the highest mountain in Lower Austria. To aid ascent trains leave Puchberg am Schneeberg station and, travelling at a gentle pace, make the climb of 1,218 m over a distance just under 10 km. On the journey, the traveller is able to enjoy outstanding views of the Alps before finally reaching what is the highest railway station in Austria, standing at an altitude of 1,795 m. Using diesel-powered *Salamander*-liveried railcars the climb takes 50 minutes. When steam traction is deployed, normally in the months of July and August, the journey takes 30 minutes longer. Given the gradients, up to 20 per cent, the rack/cogwheel system designed by Roman Abt is deployed to provide the necessary propulsion on the metre gauge line. This railway is one of the only three rack/cogwheel railways in Austria. The first plans for a cog railway to climb the Schneeberg go back to 1872 but a contract to build the Schneebergbahn was not awarded until 1895. In July 1897, the first section of the railway was opened from Puchberg to Baumgartner, followed three months later with the section to Hochschneeberg. The railway received Royal blessing when, in June 1902, Emperor Franz-Josef I rode on the Schneebergbahn to visit the Elisabethkirche. In 1937, the railway operation was taken over by the Bundesbahn Österreich (BBÖ) later to become the Austrian national railway, Österreichische

Schneebergbahn's *Salamander* No. 2 awaits departure at Puchberg station on 5th July, 2007.

*Author*

Bundesbahnen (ÖBB). At the beginning of 1997, the 100th anniversary of the railway, Niederösterreichische VerkehrsorganisationsgmbH. (NÖVOG) joined with ÖBB to take responsibility for the running of the cog railway although ÖBB still retains overall ownership of the facilities. The railway is open each year between the end of April and the end of October. More information can be obtained from www.schneebergbahn.at For information, the ÖBB route from Wiener Neustadt to Puchberg, a distance of 28 km, is also called the Schneebergbahn.

## A9 – Semmeringbahn

In December 1998, the Semmeringbahn was the first railway in the world to be admitted to the UNESCO World Heritage list. The route is from Gloggnitz, 85 km south-west of Vienna, to Mürzzuschlag via the Semmering Pass, a total distance of 41.7 km and taking up to 59 minutes to travel. The height difference on the route is 459 m with the maximum altitude being 898 m in the centre of the main tunnel near Semmering station. The maximum gradient is 2.5 per cent so that rack/cogwheel assistance is not required. However, some of the loads hauled are so great that extra locomotives, pilot and banking, have to be added. To achieve the height differences the line twists and turns following the natural contours and causing trains to travel almost double the 21 km that 'the crow flies'. The railway is a magnificent feat of 19th century engineering as identified by UNESCO - 'The Semmering Railway represents an outstanding technological solution to a major physical problem in the construction of early railways'. Success, however, had its human costs - falling rocks killed 14 workers in 1850 and a cholera/typhoid outbreak followed claiming more than 750 lives. On the route, there are 16 viaducts with an overall length of 1,607 m. The longest, with a length of 276 m, crosses the River Schwarza near Payerbach. The highest viaduct is the Kalte Rinne

near Breitenstein with a height of 46 m. There are 15 tunnels of which the longest are the two Semmering peak tunnels. Adverse weather, incidentally, rarely affects the railway thus allowing all year round running. The railway's history began in 1842 when an 'Imperial Edict' was issued for a railway to be built over the Semmering Pass connecting Vienna with points south and west. Dr Carl Ritter von Ghega (1802-1860), a mathematician from Vienna, was charged with exploring the feasibility and to submit proposals. It was not long before work began and by October 1844 the western section to Mürzzuschlag was opened. However, matters slowed for four years caused by a lack of confidence on how to construct the peak tunnel, there being no experience elsewhere to draw upon. However, in 1848, work re-commenced and soon the line was ready for its first trials. The requirement was that the steam locomotives should be able to 'pull 140 tons at 11.38 kmh on the steepest gradient.' The engines available at the time were not up to the task so engineers Wilhelm Freiherr von Engerth and Fischer von Röslerstamm were commissioned to produce a new design. These locomotives named after Engerth proved suitable and in July 1854 the first scheduled passenger trains crossed the Semmering. Steam continued until 1956 when a 3-year programme of electrification was pursued. The railway is one that should not be missed but be warned, there are plans for this route to be replaced by one which is not so arduous. See www.semmeringbahn.at

## A10 – Ybbstalbahn

The town of Waidhofen an der Ybbs is 25 km south of Amstetten. It is from here that the Ybbstalbahn operates two services; one to Lunz am See, a distance of 53.6 km and the other to Ybbsitz, a distance of 5.7 km. Both routes have narrow gauge (760 mm) lines and are not electrified requiring diesel-powered locomotives and railcars to be deployed, some of which are of historical interest. The

Semmering station on 8th July, 2007 as seen from near the village of Steinhaus. Note the blue and cream coloured railcar No. 5144 001-4 which is 'plinthed' alongside the memorial to Dr Carl Ritter von Ghega, the founding father of the Semmeringbahn. *Author*

line originally opened to passenger and freight traffic on 15th July, 1896 and has run successfully ever since. However, over recent times there has been a significant fall in use of the railway both for passengers and for freight. This has not been helped by the huge costs of repairing flood damage in 2007, as well as the rising costs of maintaining the infrastructure. This has prompted a proposal to curtail services. Understandably, this suggestion has led to an angry reaction from local residents many of whom are members of 'Verein Pro Ybbstalbahn', an association of supporters of the railway. As this book is being finalized the furious debate continues including a physical protest at Easter 2009. To follow progress on this issue, and perhaps lend some support, visit www.probahn.at The regular website, www.ybbstalbahn.at, is also well worth visiting especially the gallery section which helpfully illustrates what is under threat.

Ybbstalbahn's locomotive No. 2095.05 and carriages seen at Opponitz on 7th October, 2007. *Author*

## A11 – Ennstalbahn

The Ennstalbahn is an electrified single track main line operating in the states of Styria and Salzburg. It was originally part of the Empress Elizabeth Railway network – k.k. privilegierte Kaiserin-Elisabeth-Bahn. The concession to build the railway was granted in 1856. What is now called the Ennstalbahn, named after the local River Enns which it follows, was one of 18 routes within the 'k.k.' network. The first line to be completed was the Vienna to Linz route in 1858 and more lines followed over the next two decades. It was not until August 1875, however, that the Ennstalbahn was opened to traffic. The route of the railway is from Bischofshofen (alt. 544 m), 57 km south of Salzburg, to Selzthal (alt. 639 m) in Styria. The distance covered is 98.9 km and the journey normally takes about 87 minutes. Bischofshofen is a small town with a population of 10,087 and an important railway hub on the Westbahn. The town is located in a popular winter sports area and every year is the host for the final round in the legendary Four Hills ski jumping tournament on the *Paul Ausserleitner Schanze*, a hill named after an Austrian ski jumper who died in a fall here in 1952. From Bischofshofen the railway travels east with views of the Schladminger Tauern range of mountains to the south and Kemetegbirge to the north. Notable peaks include the Kochofen (1,916 m), Grumpenech (2,226 m), Kudstein (2,049 m) and the Stoderzinken (2,048 m). Continuing east the train arrives at yet another popular tourist village of Schladming at the foot of the Krubbergzinken (2,134 m) littered with its numerous ski lifts and cable cars. After travelling 80 km from Bischofshofen the train arrives at the railway junction and large village of Stainach-Irdning. Here, the Salzkammergutbahn arrives from Linz (*see entry A31*). Further down the line is the important railway hub for this region at the large village of Selzthal (population 1,852). This is the meeting point of not only the Ennstalbahn and the Salzkammergutbahn, but also the Gesäuse (*see entry A17*), the Schoberpassbahn (*see entry A20*) and the Pyhrnbahn (*see entry A30*).

ÖBB service led by electric locomotive No. 1044 122-8 heading for Selzthal on the Ennstalbahn on 9th October, 2007.

*Author*

## A12 – Giselabahn

This railway is part of Austria's main rail artery, the Westbahn. The section between Kitzbühel and Zell-am-See is called the Giselabahn. The line was opened in 1875 and was named after Emperor Franz-Josef I's eldest daughter, Gisela. The route is double track and electrified to the Austrian standard. It is a very busy line both with freight and passenger traffic. In spite of the heavy traffic on the route, part is used for 'nostalgie' excursions during the summer months. The route selected for the trips is from Hopfgarten via Kirchberg in Tirol, Kitzbühel and Saalfelden to Zell am See, a total distance of 83 km. The service operates on Tuesdays from the end of May to mid-September. (NB: It is necessary to book a reservation at the Kirchberg Tourist Office the day before departure.) The excursion consumes the whole day and includes a three hour stay in Zell am See before returning by bus to Hopfgarten. Included in the train on this 'nostalgie' run is an original 1910-built Imperial and Royal post carriage. As a souvenir, a special postmark is franked on letters or postcards which are posted on the train. This journey on the ÖBB main line, part of the original route of the 'Orient Express' from Paris to Istanbul, is worthwhile irrespective of the excursion. The journey along the Brixen valley with the Wilder Kaiser range as the background, and further down the Kitzbühelen Alpen range, is superb. The destination Zell am See (population 9,967) is a delightful small town on the shores of the lake of the same name. There are boat excursions on the lake and the Pinzgaubahn (*see next entry*) runs from here. For more information about the excursion, consult the website www.kitzalps.com/en/nostalgia-train-giselabahn.html

## A13 – Pinzgaubahn

The Pinzgaubahn is a single track narrow gauge (760 mm) railway (de. *lokalbahn*) running from Zell am See, on the main Westbahn, to Krimml, the end of the line, 52.7 km to the east. It had been hoped at one stage that the railway would have continued to the nearby famous Krimml waterfalls (well-worth visiting) and perhaps to join with the Zillertalbahn at Mayrhofen. What a joy that would have been! The railway line follows the River Salzach all of the way down the Pinzgau valley. The line opened to traffic, mainly for timber transport, in January 1898 and was operated by the then Imperial Royal Austrian State Railways (k.k.St.B). Steam locomotives were the order of the day and a preserved example is plinthed at Mittersill station. Steam traction continued until 1964 running alongside diesel traction which had been first introduced in 1936. Freight ceased in 1998 but since November 2008 that has been resumed. Given its close proximity to the river the railway has regularly encountered flooding difficulties throughout its history. There was a particularly bad experience in 1987. In July 2005, there was another bad flood which led to the closure of nearly half the line beyond Mittersill to Krimml. Unfortunately, in that same month, the railway experienced its worst ever accident. Just prior to the floods, two locomotives with passenger trains collided head-on near Bramberg. One of the train drivers and a passenger were killed and many were injured, some of them seriously. Human error was said to be the cause. Given its difficulties, the future of the railway became precarious. In 2000, ÖBB had attempted to close the line permanently and replace it with bus services. However, the line hung on. In January 2007, an agreement was made between ÖBB and the Salzburg state for the re-construction of the track with improved dams to divert flood waters. In July 2008, the railway became 'SLB Pinzgauer Lokalbahn' as part of Salzburg AG, which already operates the Salzburger Lokalbahn services and the Schafbergbahn (*see entry A32*). This fresh impetus has brought renewed hope. It is now thought that services will be resumed on the entire line by the end of 2009 with an exciting new timetable. This railway is also active between May and October each year with steam 'nostalgie excursions'. The Austrian enthusiasts association, Club 760 (www.club760.at) is currently re-furbishing a former Yugoslavian steam locomotive which it intends to deploy on the line in 2010. For more information, see www.pinzgauerlokalbahn.at

At St Johann in Tirol station on 10th March, 2009 ÖBB railcar No. 4024 110-1 approaches. *Author*

ÖBB railcar No. 5090 002-6 at Mittersill station on 27th June, 2007.

*Author*

## A14 – Tauernbahn

The Tauernbahn runs between Schwarzach–St Veit in Salzburg State and Spittal an der Drau in Carinthia, a distance just short of 80 km although some commentators say that the named route actually travels all the way to Villach, a further 30 km. The railway is main line for all of its route and is a combination of single and double track with passing points. The key figure in the construction of the railway was Karl Wurmb (1850-1907) who was instrumental in building a number of other Austrian railways including the Murtalbahn (*see entry A18*). The establishment of the full length of the Tauernbahn was dependent on making the rail connections over the Sohlstollens to allow for the building of the Tauern tunnel. Construction of the tunnel began in 1901 and was completed in 1906. It was electrified in 1925. The tunnel burrows under the magnificent mountains of the Tauern range, i.e. the Gamskarspitze (2,833 m), the Romantenspitze (2,696 m), the Hoher Tauern (2,459 m), Kreuzkogel (2,686 m) and the Maresenspitze (2,916 m), all of these peaks being within 5 km or less of the tunnel. The tunnel is between Mallnitz-Obervellach (alt. 1,182 m) on the south side and Böckstein (alt. 1,173 m) to the north. The overall length is 8.37 km and it takes 11 minutes for a train to pass through. The tunnel experiences a considerable amount of traffic with not only long-distance passenger and freight services but also local car-carrying trains making the short hop between Mallnitz-Obervellach and Böckstein. This service saves a significant amount of difficult road travel. Less than 3 km south of Mallnitz-Obervellach a second tunnel is encountered, the Kaponig. It is 5.096 km long after which trains emerge on to the spectacular 98 m-long Kaponigrabben bridge before disappearing again into another tunnel, the 690 m-long Ochenig. After leaving this tunnel and within a few minutes, the splendid Oberfalkenstein Castle can be seen. From here, the route, which now has double track, enjoys open scenery all the way to Villach. From Spittal an der Drau, where there is the Florentine-style Porcia Castle, the railway follows the River Drau for the remainder of the journey through the Villacher Alps.

ÖBB service on the Tauernbahn alongside the River Drau heads for Villach on 9th July, 2007.           *Author*

Club U44's 1949 Duro Banavic-built No. 83.180 awaits departure on a Sunday morning excursion on 14th October, 2007.    *Author*

## A15 – Feistritztalbahn Betriebsgesellschaft

Between Weiz and Birkfeld in Styria, is a heritage railway, operated by Club U44, utilising steam traction. The club comprises a group of railway enthusiasts who came together in 1972. On Sundays between late June and late October steam trains travel over the 24 km of single narrow gauge track (760 mm). Much of the journey is alongside the River Feistritz which it follows for more than half of the route. Trains are run on some other days during the summer, detail of which can be found at www.feistritztalbahn.at The history of the railway goes back to 1909 when a plan was proposed to build a rail connection from the town of Weiz with a quarry at Birkfeld. A contract was awarded to construct the line and by December 1911 it was fully operational. Shortly after the original opening thoughts were given to extending the line a further 25 km to Rettenegg where brown coal deposits had been found. A shortage of capital to build the extension led to a decision to use forced labour, this part of the country being under Italian occupation during World War I. However, construction work eventually stopped and did not resume until another local mining company built a shorter line to Ratten. But the lack of professionalism in building the line led to it failing to receive a licence to operate. Not to be put off by officialdom, the line operated illegally carrying miners in dangerous un-braked passenger carriages. Matters improved after AG Weiz -Birkfeld took over and, after making the necessary repairs, received a licence to operate in 1930. However, the line was never profitable and the extended line was later closed. Today, freight trains still run on the 13 km stretch between Weiz and Anger. The section from Anger to Birkfeld, where this enthusiasts' workshops and engine shed are located, is only used for steam excursions. The section beyond Birkfeld to Ratten has been converted to a green-route cycleway. This is an extremely well run heritage railway utilizing interesting, well maintained, traction and rolling stock. Philatelists can combine their interest with heritage railways by buying a postage stamp which depicts one of the railway's steam locomotives.

### A16 – Erzbergbahn

Another enthusiasts' railway, 'Verein Erzbergbahn' (Erzberg Railway Association) operates from Vordernberg Markt, 67 km northwest of Graz, to Eisenerz, distance of 18.1 km on standard gauge track. A railway between Leoben, a centre of the iron industry, and Vordernberg opened in 1872 and a year later, a section between Hieflau and Eisenerz was constructed. However, the centre section between Eisenerz and Vordernberg was not built until 1891. The prime function of the railway was the transportation of iron-ore from the Erzberg mountain over the Präbichl pass to the steelworks in Vordernberg. From there the iron/steel products would travel to Leoben on the Neumarkt Sattel main line. Originally, the line utilized the Abt rack/cogwheel system to climb and, more importantly, brake the descent of the heavily laden ore wagons down the 7.2 per cent gradient. In 1980, the rack was removed making it possible for diesel-powered locomotives and railcars to operate, albeit with strengthened braking systems. In 1988, ÖBB closed the line. Fortunately two years later, and before the track had been taken up, an association of local enthusiasts was able to lease the line for a museum railway. In 2003, the association managed to find sufficient capital to purchase the railway and several buildings including the depot at Vordernberg and the station at Erzberg. In 1990, the railway opened, for the first time, to tourist traffic. It now operates on Sundays from the beginning of July to mid-September. Verein Erzbergbahn also maintains a museum of interesting railway artefacts including a cogwheel engine and a driver's cab from a steam locomotive. Preserved, but not operational, is steam locomotive No. 297 401, said to be one of the world's strongest rack locomotives. It is now on a plinth outside the museum at Vordernberg Markt station. It had originally entered service in 1942 and was finally withdrawn in 1968. Its sister locomotive, No. 297 402, had a very short life. It also entered service in January 1942 but was scrapped in 1949 with many of the parts retained to keep 297 401 going. Another steam locomotive, No. 97 217, is plinthed in the square of Vordernberg Markt close to the approach to the station. For more see www.erzbergbahn.at

Steam locomotive No. 97.217 'plinthed' in Vordernberg Markt square as photographed on 8th July, 2007. *Author*

### A17 – Gesäuse

Gesäuse is the name given to an Austrian National Park in the Ennstaler Alps as well as a valley and the delightful railway running between Selzthal and Hieflau. The distance covered is 50 km and completed by train in 39 minutes, much too short a time many say to appreciate fully the splendour of this region! Travelling north from Selzthal the electrified double track is shared with the Pyhrnbahn (*see*

Gesäuse valley on 10th October, 2007.                    *Author*

*entry A30*) but within 4 km, near to the village of Ardning, the route divides. A single track, still electrified, heads off east down the Gesäuse valley keeping the River Enns for company. Passing through the station of Frauenberg the attractive village of Admont is reached. Since 1977, Admont (population 2,850) holds the annual Admonter music festival, attracting visitors from all over Europe. A beautiful Benedictine monastery is located here, founded in 1074, which houses the world's biggest monastic library as well as an important scientific collection. Furthermore, the column of the Virgin Mary (1712), the Leopoldinenbrunnen well (1892) and Schloss Röthelstein – a castle said to be Europe's most beautiful youth hostel - are all cultural delights well worth a visit. Trains continue on to Gesäuse Eingang where they soon enter a short tunnel (238 m) from which they emerge and immediately cross a girder bridge with the fast flowing, sometimes wild river beneath. Here the mountains of Gr Buckstein (2,224 m), Kl Buchstein (1,990 m), Reichenstein (2,221 m), Hochtor (2,369 m) and the Hochzinöd (2,191 m) on either side of the valley form a high wall to the gorge which continues for 17 km down a minor gradient to the small village of Hieflau (population 873). Hieflau is where the now discontinued Eisenerzbahn used to terminate. It is from here that the railway heads north towards Weissenbach St Gallen and Kleinreifling with its route name now restored to Ennstalbahn.

### A18 – Murtalbahn

The Murtalbahn's origins go back to the rapid railway expansion of the late 19th century. In 1892, the Styrian Parliament granted approval for a railway between Unzmarkt and Mauterndorf. Construction work began in August 1893 and, within an incredible 316 days, the 76 km line was laid along with the building of 12 stations, 14 halts, offices and workshops at Murau and engine sheds at Unzmarkt, Murau and Mauterndorf. A new method of communication was installed with telephones replacing Morse

Murtalbahn rolling stock at Murau Stolzalpe station on 7th July, 2007.

*Author*

telegraphy. At first, the railway did not meet expectations particularly for the movement of felled wood as it was still considered cheaper to continue rafting the timber down the River Mur. Happily, the fortunes of the railway company improved and there were plans to extend the line to Unterweissburg but World War I put a stop to that. The war had an effect of reducing the number of train services because of coal shortages, a situation that continued after the war and only partly relieved by changing to peat burning. As elsewhere in the world, the 1930s Depression caused heavy losses to the railway. During World War II, surprisingly perhaps, passenger numbers increased and, in 1943, an extra steam locomotive had to be drafted in to help out. The positive situation, however, was not sustained after the war with the increasing popularity of road transport. By the beginning of the 1960s, the situation was desperate. The response was to implement a modernization plan bringing an end to steam in 1967. Declining passenger numbers also closed the 12 km Tamsweg to Mauterndorf section of the line. (This section, incidentally, is now actively used as an enthusiasts' railway - the Taurachbahn.) Notwithstanding this closure, the remainder of the route has since flourished with the acquisition of a modern fleet of railcars and the installation of equipment at Unzmarkt to ease the transfer of freight from the railway's 760 mm narrow gauge to standard gauge vehicles. It is estimated that in excess of 430,000 people are now transported every year and, with timber and other freight, has made today's Murtalbahn a viable concern. Fortunately, in the 1960s local enthusiasts (www.club760.at) as well as the railway's management were reluctant to abandon completely steam traction. Consequently, steam-hauled excursions were maintained and have been an important part of the annual timetable ever since and an important source of revenue to support other aspects of the railway's services. For more see www.stlb.at

## A19 – Rudolfbahn

The Rudolfbahn is also known as the Neumarkter Sattel. The latter is the name of a pass (alt. 894 m) in Styria between the Mur and the Gurktal valleys at the foot of the Kreuzeck (1,459 m) and the Kalkberg (1,591 m) mountains south-east of Unzmarkt. The pass has a long history and was very important, for example, to the Romans for passsage between southern Carinthia and Upper Austria.The full main line route is from Bruck an de Mur to St Veit an der Glan. At St Veit an der Glan, where the Hochosterwitz Castle dominates the town, the route divides with a double track line going down to Klagenfurt and a single track line running along the Ossiacher See to Villach. On this route, the ruins of the Roman-built Landskron Castle can be appreciated. However, the part of the route that is generally accepted gives its name to this railway, is that section from Leoben to Klagenfurt via St Michael, Knittelfeld, Unzmarkt and Treibach-Althofen, a total distance of 150 km. The concession to build the railway, which became known as the 'Kronprinz-Rudolf-Bahn', was granted in 1866. No time was wasted in the construction and by 1868 the progress of the line had proceeded rapidly and well. The long section from St Michael to Villach via Unzmarkt was opened in the October followed by the Leoben to St Michael section in the December. The next year saw the connection between St Veit an der Glan and Klagenfurt opened. After a promising start, the impact of the Austria's financial crisis of 1873, part of a worldwide problem, hit the railway badly. In 1880, it went into administration and finally was nationalized in 1884. Although it is well over 100 years since it lost its independence, the railway retains its original name, the 'Rudolfbahn'. The town of Knittelfeld (population 12,740) on the route is an important maintenance centre for ÖBB. Located there is also an interesting railway museum see www.knittelfeld.at/informationen_service/eisenbahnmuseum For information, near Zeltweg, the Österreichring can be found where the Austrian F1 Grand Prix events were run between 1970 and 1987 and again between 1997 and 2003.

A class '1044' heads a passenger service for St Michael seen here crossing the River Mur at Preg on 11th October, 2007. *Author*

## A20 – Schoberpassbahn

The Schober Pass in Styria, at an altitude of 849 m, is the lowest pass in the Alps. The pass separates the Tauern Niedere from the Eisenerzer Alps and forms the watershed between the Enns and Mur rivers. The pass has always been a major route and since the late 19th century has also had the benefit of a railway. The route the railway takes is from the important rail hub at Selzthal and travels east-south-east to St Michael, a total distance of 63 km. It only has a double track for some of the way. Indeed, in railway circles the name Schober has become synonymous with 'bad traffic route' because of the many bottlenecks encountered. The line was not electrified until 1964. Trains leave Selzthal and travel down a beautiful wide valley keeping close to the River Palten until reaching Wald am Schoberpass, a small village of 645 inhabitants and the highest point on the pass almost half way to St Michael. Wald am Schoberpass station is where there is an important, indeed critical passing loop. The Palten diverts to its source near here and a little further down the line the River Liesing meets the railway from its source on the Himmeleck mountain (alt. 2,096 m). The railway continues through the Unterwald tunnel (1,075 m) to the villages of Kalwang (population 1,200), Mautern, a former toll village (population 2,000), Seiz and Traboch-Timmersdorf before reaching St Michael. At St Michael is the rail junction of this line with the Rudolfbahn -Neumarkter Sattel (*see previous entry*).

## A21 – Peggau - Übelbach

Steiermärkische Landesbahnen, a Graz-based railway company, operates a number of rail routes in Styria. A short, but nonetheless delightful, route runs between Peggau and Übelbach. Peggau is 21 km north of Graz and 20 km south of Mixnitz. The line is 10.25 km long with a standard gauge and electrified to the 15kV AC

ÖBB railcar No. 4024 002-0 approaches Wald am Schoberpaß on 10th October, 2007. *Author*

Übelbach station on 12th October, 2007 with railcar No. Bde 4/4 593 and BDt 994 awaiting departure. *Author*

standard. Peggau-Deutschfeistritz, to give the village its full name, is a combined village. It has a population of about 6,000 people whose homes are divided either side of the River Mur. Peggau-Deutschfeistritz is a main line station on that section of the Südbahn from Bruck an der Mur to Graz. The lesser mountains of Hochtrötsch (1,239 m), Burgstaller Höhe (1,218 m), Schöckl (1,445 m) and Hohe Rannach (1,018 m) dominate the village to the east. The line to Übelbach (population 2,037) follows the river of the same name that traces its source to the nearby Speikkogel (1,988 m). Other mountains which enclose the village include the Mühlbacher Kogel (1,050 m), Schererkogel (1,218 m), Sadningkogel (1,449 m) and the Fuchskogel (1,293 m). Übelbach is in the Graz-Umgebung district known for its many volcanic peaks and is a popular tourist resort. There are natural springs locally known as 'Johannisbrunnen' found in local wells. The waters from these wells were analysed in the 18th century by Professor Heinrich von Crantz, personal physician to Empress Maria Theresa, and declared to have significant healing properties. There are regular visits to the wells organized by the local tourist office. A landmark in the village is a beautiful church with spire. The rail journey through the villages of Prenning, Waldstein and Guggenbach takes 28 minutes. For more information, see www.stlb.at

## A22 – Achenseebahn

Travelling north-east along the motorway from Innsbruck, after 39 km one comes to the town of Jenbach (population 6,896). In railway terms, Jenbach station is unusual, indeed unique in Austria, in that railway lines of three different gauges converge, i.e. standard, 760 mm and metre. This distinction is shared with Montreux in Switzerland (*see entry CH10*). The main line running from Innsbruck over the border near Kufstein to Rosenheim in Germany (*see entry D18*) is standard gauge. The Zillertalbahn (*see entry A29*) which runs to the ski resort of Mayrhofen is 760 mm gauge. Finally, there is this railway which is metre gauge. The Achenseebahn is said to be Europe's oldest steam-operated cog railway. Emperor Franz-Josef I granted approval in 1888 for this 6.7 km-long railway to be constructed between Jenbach and Achensee. It took less than a year to build the tracks stopping 400 m short of the lake's landing stage. This was a deliberate decision to allow the local monastery to earn income by providing a human 'escalator' to transport luggage and goods to and from the trains and the steamboats. This arrangement came to a halt in 1916 when the military extended the track to the landing stage. Steam locomotives with inclined boilers capable of driving both the wheels and the cogs were introduced at the outset. There was a brief flirtation with electrification during World War I but it has been steam-operated ever since. The original rôle of the railway was to transport felled wood. However, during World War II, it assumed a vital role in transporting over 140,000 refugees escaping from Allied bombings. Between Jenbach and the village of Eben, a distance of 3.6 km, trains negotiate a 16 per cent gradient by employing Riggenbach's rack/cogwheel system. Thereafter, and to the landing stage, normal adhesion suffices. The railway operates frequent services every day between May and October with each journey taking an enjoyable 45 minutes. The railway recently experienced a catastrophic fire at its Jenbach engine shed destroying sadly the 1899-built locomotive No. 1 *Eben am Achensee*. The two other 1899-built locomotives, No. 2 *Jenbach* and No. 3 *Achenkirch*, have survived and a third, No. 4 was brought back into service in April 2009. The excellent website (in 12 languages!) is well worth visiting as is, of course, the railway - www.achenseebahn.at

Achenseebahn's 1899-built cogwheel locomotive No. 2 *Jenbach* leaving Jenbach station on 27th June, 2007. *Author*

## A23 – Arlbergbahn

The Arlbergbahn connecting Innsbruck and Bludenz, is Austria's only east to west mountain railway. The route, almost 136 km in length, is said to be Europe's most difficult mountain railway because of the ever-present threat of avalanches, mudflows, rockfalls and floods. The line is operated by ÖBB and is used by international trains and was, until June 2007, part of the Orient Express route to Vienna. As early as 1842 ideas for this railway were being discussed to meet the British requirement for a route from England to India. However, the technical diffculties of negotiating the Arlberg were considered too great to make construction viable. Following the pioneering construction and opening of the Semmeringbahn in 1854 (*see entry A9*) the situation changed showing that the potential problems could be overcome. Construction began in 1880 and within only four years the line was completed, including the 10.25 km-long Arlberg tunnel. Sadly, the construction of the tunnel alone accounted for the loss of 92 lives. Initially, only one track ran through the tunnel but with the rapid growth in traffic, by 1885 a second track had been installed. Steam-hauled trains were deployed from the outset but unfortunately their use in the tunnels brought unintended consequences. Passengers and staff increasingly suffered breathing problems and so by the mid-1920s it was decided that electrification should be introduced. The railway is part of Austria's Westbahn and is a combination of single and double tracks. The route, electrified at 15kV AC, allows the most powerful locomotives to operate. The year 2008 saw the introduction of ÖBB's Railjet services that have already made significant reductions in journey times. There are a number of notable structures on the route. Perhaps the best known, west of Pians near Landeck, is the 232 m-long Trissanabrücke steel viaduct which crosses the river 80 m below. The Wiesberg castle can be seen nearby. For the 2001 World Ski Championships the railway station at St Anton on the eastern side of the Arlberg tunnel was completely reconstructed and the tunnel itself lengthened a few metres.

## A24 – Brennerbahn

The Brennerbahn runs between Innsbruck and Verona in Italy, a distance of 272 km. To achieve this journey the Brenner Pass (alt. 1,371 m), the lowest international crossing across the Alps, has to be negotiated. The route is an important part of the Berlin to Palermo connection, perhaps the longest north to south railway line in Europe. For centuries this crossing has been used by travellers. The Romans regularized it in the 2nd century AD by building one of their renowned roads. However, for years to come, the traffic was restricted to mule trains and carts. In 1777, that changed with the building of a road surface which could take carriages. Ninety years later, the railway followed. Since the end of World War I control of Brenner (it. Brennero) has been shared between Austria and Italy, prior to that it was part of the Austrian-Hungarian Empire. Incidentally, in March 1940, Hitler and Mussolini met at Brenner to celebrate their  axis 'Pact of Steel'. The roadway up to the Brenner pass is always busy and some attempt to relieve the congestion and related pollution has been gained by encouraging heavy goods vehicles to let the 'train take the strain'. The motorway, which incidentally can be seen from the train for almost all of the way, features the 'Europabrücke' viaduct located a few kilometres north of the Brenner Pass. It is a large concrete bridge carrying the six-lane motorway over the River Sill valley. At a height of 180 m and a length of 820 m, it is celebrated as a masterpiece of modern engineering; it was completed in 1963. The Brennerbahn has the distinction of being the only main line railway crossing the Alps in the open. However, that will change when eventually the Brenner base tunnel is opened. For more information on this go to the Brennerbahn entry in the chapter on Italy (*see entry I19*).

Near Telfs on the Arlbergbahn is an ÖBB passenger service hauled by electric locomotive No. 1044.111 on 26th June, 2007.    *Author*

The Brennerbahn near Gries on 10th March, 2009. The railway is on the left of the valley and the motorway on the right. *Author*

IVB tram No. 88 at Fulpmes station on 26th June, 2007.    *Author*

## A25 – Innsbruck Tramways

Innsbrucker Verkehrsbetriebe und Stubaitalbahn GmbH, IVB for short, is the company which operates Innsbruck's three city tram routes and two light railways - the Stubaitalbahn and the Mittelgebirgsbahn. The Innsbruck tram network totals 17.6 km operating on an electricity power supply of 600V DC. The depot for the tramway is located at Wilthen. Near to the depot is the Tiroler Museumbahnen which safeguards a large collection of trams and related material. A delightful hour-long tour of the city centre on an 'oldtimer' tram is included in the visit to the museum. The Stubaitalbahn is a single track metre gauge light railway which travels from Innsbruck (alt. 582 m) to the resort of Fulpmes (alt. 936 m) a distance of 18.2 km. From Fulpmes a road travels to the enormous Stubai glacier, a popular year-round skiing area. It is accessible by a funicular from Mutterbergalm. The journey on the electric tram-railcars, powered by an 800V DC electricity supply, takes 60 minutes. The gradients never exceed 4.5 per cent so rack/cogwheel assistance is not required. The Stubaitalbahn operates frequent daily services all the year round. It has been part of IVB since 1997. The Mittelgebirgsbahn is a metre gauge light railway on which electrically powered (800V DC) tram-railcars travel from the Bergisel station at the south end of Innsbruck up to the winter/summer resort of Igls, a distance of 8.3 km. The altitude difference between the two termini is 278 m but the trams negotiate this, avoiding rack/cogwheel assistance, by taking a circuitous route! The journey takes 25 minutes. The Mittelgebirgsbahn was originally opened to the public in the mid-summer of 1900. From the outset and for the following 36 years the trains were steam-hauled using Krauss-built 0-6-2T tank engines. Four of the carriages used during those times have been beautifully preserved and can be seen in the Tiroler Museumsbahnen. The views from both the Stubaitalbahn and the Mittelgebirgsbahn of the city of Innsbruck and its prominent Wilton Abbey Church and the Nordkette slopes of the Karwendel mountains behind are superb. For more information, see www.ivb.at

## A26 – Karwendelbahn/Mittenwaldbahn

Karwendelbahn is a single track standard gauge electrified railway running from Innsbruck to the Austrian-German border located between Scharnitz and Mittenwald. At the border the railway's name is changed to Mittenwaldbahn (*see entry D9*). The distance from Innsbruck to the border is 33.2 km and a further 5 km to Mittenwald. A typical journey from Innsbruck to Scharnitz takes 49 minutes and an added 32 minutes to reach the final destination of Garmish-Partenkirchen. The journey up from Innsbruck is superb. Indeed, it is equally pleasurable by road. On leaving Innsbruck (alt. 582 m) the railway heads west on the main Arlbergbahn and within one kilometre cuts right. Just before Kranebitten it enters its first tunnel, 214 m long, followed by a further two more tunnels of shorter lengths. Beyond Martinswand, the longest tunnel is encountered, 1.8 km in length. The train continues up to and beyond Hochzirl (alt. 922 m) where it makes a 180º loop through three tunnels in the mountainside before continuing to the village of Leithen (alt. 1,054 m). So far on this 11 km route there have been 15 tunnels. The maximum gradient has been 3.8 per cent, trains achieving this without rack/cogwheel assistance. The line continues to climb and eventually arrives at Seefeld in Tirol (alt. 1,182 m) which is the highest point on this route and 22.4 km from Innsbruck. Seefeld in Tirol is a popular tourist resort especially for enjoying the Seefelder Spitze mountain (2,221 m). To assist in the climb there is the Roßhuttebahn, a cable-hauled railcar which gains 811 m in height and to within 157 m of the summit. The views from the top are breathtaking. A further 11 km further on, the train arrives at the village of Scharnitz. One cannot miss the station – the walls are painted a vivid bright green!

## A27 – Außerfernbahn

The Außerfernbahn is a single track railway in the northern Tyrol. It is completely independent from the rest of the Austrian Federal Railways (ÖBB) network as access is only possible by travelling on German tracks. Constructed between 1905 and 1912, the 44 km route starts at the western German-Austrian border (de. Staatsgrenze) between Pfronten-Steinach and Schönbichl and concludes at the Austrian-German border between Schober and Griesen. The railway before Pfronten-Steinach comes from Kempten via Nesselwang (*see entry D3*) and after Schober travels to Garmisch-Partenkirchen (*see entry D4*). The route from Pfronten is not electrified but becomes so once it reaches the market town of Reutte in Tirol (population 5,738). Thereafter it operates at 15kV AC all the way to Garmisch-Partenkirchen. Up until 2001, the responsibility for the Außerfernbahn was shared between ÖBB and Deutsche Bahn (DB) but since then the latter has taken full responsibility for the entire route including the Austrian section as delegated to them by the State of Tyrol. The railway has been described as a jewel in Tyrol's crown and when one travels this journey it is not difficult to see why. Sandwiched between the Lechtaler and the Ammergauer Alps the scenery is superb with at least seven mountain lakes, notably the Halerwanger See, the Plansee (in winter a natural ice rink) and the Eibsee. There are numerous high peaks most rising to at least 2,000 m. Standing above Reutte is the Gr Schlicke (2,059 m), Säuling (2,048 m) and the Thaneller (2,341 m). Further east is the Kohlbergspitze (2,202 m), Bleispitze (2,255 m) and the Daniel (2,340 m). Eventually the traveller reaches the crowning glory of the region, the Zugspitze (2,962 m) the highest peak in Germany located on the German-Austrian border. A rack/cogwheel runs up the Zugspitze (*see entry D5*). Tourism is taken very seriously here both by the Austrians and the Germans. For example, embracing territory in both countries is

A DB service approaches Kranebitten station on 21st October, 2007.

*Author*

DB Regio service on the Außerfernbahn near Reutte on 23rd October, 2007.
*Author*

the Zugspitzarena, which offers 300 km of hiking trails and 1,000 km of mountain bike routes. There is even a 9-hole golf course! A website for more information is www.erlebnisbahn.at/ausserfernbahn

### A28 – Serfauser Alpen-U-Bahn

Serfauser Alpen U-bahn, also known as the Dorfbahn Serfaus, is a unique underground railway, a most unusual find in a mountainous area! The U-Bahn is located in the village of Serfaus, 28 km south of Landeck. Serfaus is a busy Tyrolean ski resort, which, in the winter months, caters for large numbers of skiers. The ski slopes are accessible by a cable car as well as by a gondola lift. The lower ski stations are located at the far end of the village's main street with the Dorfbahn Serfaus operating a shuttle service to them from the large car parks on the approach to the village from Landeck. The U-Bahn allows the narrow village streets to be car-free, a situation similar to that which applies in Zermatt in

Switzerland. The line, built in 1985 by the Freissler-Otis company, consists of a 1,280 m-long single track, with just one train operating on a regular shuttle basis. The maximum gradient travelled is 5.3 per cent. The train comprises two cars carried on an air cushion and moved by a funicular haulage system. The tunnel is three metres wide and just over three metres high. The train can carry up to 270 people at any one time and travels at a speed of up to 40 kmh. All year round services operate and the journey is free of charge. For more information, see www.serfaus-fiss-ladis.at

### A29 – Zillertalbahn

Perhaps one of the best-known railways in Austria is the world-famous Zillertalbahn. It runs from Jenbach, 39 km north-east of Innsbruck, where the OBB main line and the Achenseebahn (*see entry A22*) are co-located. The single track narrow gauge (760 mm) non-electrified line runs on an attractive 32 km route to the resort of Mayrhofen (population 3,869) close to the Hintertux glacier (3,250 m). The railway, first opened to traffic in July 1902, nowadays delivers its services using modern diesel-powered railcars taking 56 minutes for the journey. However, steam hauled services – usually three a day - are operated between early May and late October. At Christmas and in some winter months, steam 'specials' are also run. The steam trains take a delicious 80 minutes and are immensely popular. The railway maintains four steam locomotives of early 20th century vintage carrying the evocative names of *Zillertal, Tirol, Gerlos* and *Hobbylok*. The railway enthusiasts' Club 760 (*see entry A18*) also keeps a 1909-built Krauss-Linz steam locomotive on this railway. Both the diesel railcars and the steam locomotives operate without rack/cogwheel assistance as the altitude rises less than 100 m over the entire route. As a matter of interest to UK rail enthusiasts is that some of the Zillertalbahn's surplus rolling stock was sold some years ago to the Welshpool and Llanfair Light Railway in Wales. The run down the Ziller valley,

The 'village' terminus of the Serfauser Alpen-U-Bahn on 22nd October, 2007.

*Author*

following the river with the Tuxer Alps to the west and the Kitzbüheler Alps to the east and heading for the majestic Zillertal Alps, is nothing but superb. Facing the traveller are the Mittl Grinbergspitze (2,867 m), Dristner (2,760 m) and the Ahornspitze (2,973 m) mountains which together form a massive wall at the end of the line. Mayrhofen is popular all the year round but especially so in winter for its skiing with pistes of varying degrees of difficulty to suit both the novice and the expert. There is a particularly long steep (red) run on the Ahorn which was on the World Cup downhill circuit but was removed as it was considered too dangerous! Incidentally, the Ahornbahn cable car has gondolas which can transport up to 160 people and as such are the biggest in Austria. For more information see www.zillertalbahn.at

### A30 – Pyhrnbahn

The Pyhrnbahn is the name given to the 104 km route from Linz to Selzthal and which, when completed, became one of the last critical links in Austria's national rail network. The northernmost part of the route was originally built as the Krems Valley Railway in the 1880s. In 1881, the Linz to Kremsmünster line was opened followed by sections to Micheldorf in 1883 and to Klaus in 1888. Klaus (alt. 476 m) lies on the banks of the River Steyr at the foot of the Sengsengebirge mountains, which, for the purpose of this book, is where this railway's defined Alps begin. In 1901, a law was enacted giving approval for state funding for the Tauernbahn, Karawankenbahn, Wocheinerbahn (*see entry SLO2*), Wechselbahn and the Pyhrnbahn. This legislation allowed for the building of the Bosruck tunnel (begun 1901), the line from Klaus through the Bosruck tunnel to Selzthal (begun 1903), a refurbishment of the former Krems Valley railway to Linz (begun 1904) and a new path between Micheldorf and Klaus (begun 1905). By August 1906, the route was complete. In the early 1960s, the Bosruck tunnel had to be renovated because of rock pressure, water ingress and smoke damage.

Zillertalbahn's No. 3 *Tirol* crosses the plain from Jenbach heading for Mayrhofen on 27th June, 2007. *Author*

On the Pyhrnbahn is ÖBB's electric locomotive No. 1044 058-4 about to enter the Bosruck tunnel on 10th October, 2007. *Author*

Once renovation work was completed, diesel traction operated until the line was electrified in 1977. The route from Klaus to Selzthal, via Spital am Pyhrn, is 44 km long and single track all the way with gradients never exceeding two per cent. After Spital am Pyhrn, the highest mountain on the route will be seen, the Gr Pyhrgas (2,244 m) before entering the 4.767 km long tunnel burrowing under the Bosruck mountain (1,976 m). The route then passes through the village of Ardning and within a short distance, at Selzthal Nord, it meets the Gesäuse line for the shallow descent into Selzthal.

## A31 – Salzkammergutbahn

The Salzkammergut is a single track electrified railway running between Attnang-Puchheim on the Westbahn in the Upper Austria state and Stainach-Irdning in Styria. At Stainach-Irdning the line connects with the Bischofshofen-Selzthal route, the Ennstalbahn (*see entry A11*). The railway traces its origins back to the 1870s when the engineer Carl Freiherr von Schwarz, working for the k.k. priv-Ischl Ebensee Steger railway company, began the construction of the line between Ebensee and Steeg. This line would effectively connect the Traunsee with the Hallstättersee lakes, which at the time, were used by boats for the transport of salt. It was for this new railway to assist that transportation. The route, linked with the development of the Rudolfbahn (*see entry A19*) was completed in 1877. The line from Attnang-Puchheim (alt. 415 m) to Stainach-Irdning takes a pleasant meandering route following the Aurach and Traun rivers and skirting the Traunsee from Gmunden to Ebensee before arriving at Bad Ischl. This 'salt' town has a long history and is especially noted as the location of the former summer residence of Emperor Franz-Josef I (1830-1916). The parents of Franz-Josef had not been blessed with children so their doctor advised them to take advantage of the mineral salt baths in the town. It worked, and Franz-Josef was born. He and his later brothers soon became known as the 'Salt Princes', their existence

linking directly to the waters of Bad Ischl. The route continues passing the Hallstättersee to the village of Obertraun-Dachsteinhöhlen and on to Bad Aussee (population 5,086). Bad Aussee is the geographic mid-point of Austria, a fact which is marked by a stone monument in the town centre. Surrounded by five lakes as well as the mountains, the town is a popular resort and spa. Continuing alongside the River Kainishtraun, the line arrives at Bad Mittendorf (alt. 820 m) which is the highest point on the line and famous as a location for the World Cup Ski Jumping tour. The next village reached, where the line meets the River Grimming, is Tauplitz (population 1,012) popular for its winter skiing on the Tauplitzalm (1,656 m), before dropping down into Stainach-Irdning. The total distance covered by the route is 107.6 km. The mountain ranges that the trains pass include the Höllegebirge (high point Gr Hollkogel – 1,862 m) and Totes Gebirge (high point the Schönberg – 2,093 m). For more detail, see www.salzkammergutbahn.net Incidentally, when travelling this route do not be surprised if the scenery evokes memories of 'The Sound of Music'. Many of the scenes in the film were shot here.

## A32 – Schafbergbahn

Located at St Wolfgang, 29 km south-east by road from Salzburg, is the Schafbergbahn, which started life out in 1893. It claims to be the steepest steam driven rack/cogwheel railway in Austria. The track is metre gauge and, because of gradients of up to 25.5 per cent, the Roman Abt-designed rack/cogwheel system has to be employed. The route is 5.85 km long over which trains rise 1,190 m in altitude, taking 45 minutes to reach the summit station. The railway operates six steam locomotives of 1893 and 1894 vintage, and four modern oil-fired steam engines built between 1992 and 1995, two diesel-powered railcars, 13 passenger carriages and four goods vehicles. Leaving Schafberg station, trains travel through St Wolfgang and on through meadows and forests to Dorneralpe (1,040 m) where the steam engines take

Like Emperor Franz Jozef and his family before them, these passengers embark and disembark at Bad Ischl station. This photograph was taken on 30th June, 2007.

*Author*

Cogwheel locomotive No. Z14 leaves St Wolfgang station pushing its carriages towards the Schafbergspitze on 30th June, 2007.    *Author*

water. The journey continues to the Schafbergalpe halt (1,363 m) where the energetic can disembark and, taking about an hour, hike to the summit. Those of a less athletic disposition can continue on the train for a further 10 minutes to reach the summit station at Schafbergspitze (1,732 m).The summit hosts the oldest mountain hotel in Austria built in 1862. It offers comfortable rooms but the only access is by way of the railway. The views from the Schafberg mountain (1,783 m) are considered to offer the most beautiful in the whole of the Salzkammergut region of Austria. Another part of this railway's operations is to offer boat trips. These boat services sail on the Wolfgangsee using the 1873-constructed paddle steamer *Franz-Josef I* linking the lake's ports of Kurs, Strobl, Gschwendt Parkplatz, St Wolfgang, Ried-Falkenstein, Fürberg and St Gilgen. Salzkammergutbahn GmbH now operates the railway and lake services. More detail can be found at www.schafbergbahn.at

### A33 – Montafonerbahn

The Montafonerbahn Aktiengesellschaft (MBS) is a privately owned railway company in Vorarlberg state that provides passenger services on a standard gauge line between the towns of Bludenz and Schruns, a total distance of 12.7 km. The journey takes 20 minutes. The line was built in 1905 and at that time electrified at 600V DC but nowadays the railway operates with a 15kV AC supply. From the shared station at Bludenz, trains branch off the main Arlbergbahn and head south-east keeping the River Ill company for its entire route. The railway does cross the river on one occasion on an attractive steel viaduct near to the village of Loruns. The railway has its depot and workshops at Schruns where a large collection of electric railcars of various vintages are also retained.  In the summer months, the company operates steam-hauled specials. Incidentally, the distinctive yellow and red liveried MBS rolling stock are not the only vehicles to be seen travelling on this route, ÖBB rolling stock may also be observed. Services operate on the line daily throughout the year. There

Montafonerbahn diesel railcar No. ET 10.108 crossing the steel viaduct over the River Ill on 11th July, 2007. *Author*

were thoughts to extend the existing railway by re-opening the former 18 km Vorarlberger Illwerke line to the ski resort of Partenen. This line was built using a 760 mm gauge but was closed in 1962. Once re-opened, this railway will provide an enjoyable scenic route; unfortunately, the plans have yet to materialize.

## A34 – Wälderbähnle

The Wälderbähnle in the Vorarlberg state, often referred to by its former name the Bregenzerwaldbahn, operates a heritage-tourist railway between the villages of Bezau and Bersbuch via Schwarzenberg. The route, a distance of 6 km, takes trains 23 minutes to travel. The track is 760 mm gauge and operates by adhesion only. A notable structure on the route is the Sporeneggbrücke, a 68 m-long girder viaduct. The Bregenzerwaldbahn was opened in September 1902 and ran its operations on the route from Bregenz to Bezau, a distance of 35.4 km. Unfortunately, in July 1980, there was an enormous rockslide which caused total disruption to train services on the route. In 1983, a limited service was resumed from Kennelbach to Bregenz. However, by the end of January 1985 continuing to operate the services was not considered viable. The line was finally closed. But, in the same year the 'Association Bregenzerwaldbahn Museumsbahn' was founded with the objectives of safeguarding the historic rolling stock and, where finances would permit, to restore items to working order. This it has successfully achieved and now operates an excellent and popular tourist train service. There is a well-stocked covered museum where the operational 1902-built U 25 *Bezau*, the 1902-built U 24, the 1931-built Uh 102 and other steam locomotives are stored. There are also diesel locomotives retained dating back to the 1940s together with a collection of passenger carriages and other wagons. There is a small shop which sells souvenirs. For more information, visit the website www.waelderbaehnle.at

Wälderbähnle's diesel locomotive No. 2091.08 hauls a late morning excursion over the River Bregenzerach towards Bersbuch on 12th July, 2007.                                                            *Author*

# Germany

## Introduction

The German Alps are located in a comparatively narrow strip of mountains running along Germany's southern border with Switzerland and Austria. Just one of Germany's Federal States lays claim to the Alps, Bavaria. The Bavarian Alps, as they are referred to, run from near Lindau on the shores of Lake Constance (Bodensee) in the west to Salzburg just over the border in Austria in the east.

These Alps can be divided into three sections. First, there is the western section, known as the Allgsuer Alpen, located between Lake Constance and the River Lech. Second, a central section, referred to as the Bayerische Alpen, found between the Lech and Inn rivers. Finally, a third section to the east, called the Salzburger Alpen, beginning at the River Inn and running to the Austrian border and taking in the Berchtesgaden National Park.

Bavaria has an area of 70,548 sq. km (27,200 sq. miles) and is the largest in geographical area of all the German states. It boasts a population of over 12.5 million. The State is divided into seven administrative regions known as Regierungsbezirke, two of which administer part of the Alps, Swabia (Schwaben) to the west and Upper Bavaria (de. Oberbayern) to the east. Munich (de. München) is the capital of Bavaria famous amongst other things for its beer production and, of course, its consumption at the annual 'Oktoberfest'! At the beginning of 2008, the population of the city was said to be 1,356,594. It is in the 'Bayerische Alpen' that Germany's highest peak can be found, the *Zugspitze* reaching a height above sea level of 2,962 metres.

Apart from a route from Switzerland near Lindau, all the international roads into the German Alps are from Austria. Running from west to east, they are the roads from Weißenbach, near Reutte, to Sondhofen via the Oberjoch Pass; a road from Reutte splits at the border, one going to Nasselwand and the other to Füssen; and, there is also a high mountain road from Reutte to Oberammergau. There are two routes into Garmisch-Partenkirchen, one from Imst and the other from Innsbruck. A major road and a motorway links Innsbruck with the Munich-Salzburg motorway via Kufstein. There are three crossings east of Kufstein, i.e. from Aschau to Walchsee; Schleching and Reit im Winkl both for Kössen; and, Bad Reichenhall for Lofer via the Steinpaß.

There are four international railway connections into the German Alps, again all from Austria. Those connections are from Kempten, one of the oldest towns in Germany, to Pfronten-St Stainach heading for Reutte; and, Griesen having come from Reutte and heading for Garmisch-Partenkirchen. (NB: The latter two routes are in fact linked where trains from Kempten travel to Garmisch-Partenkirchen but via the Austrian town of Reutte on the route known as the Außferfernbahn – *see also A27*.) Also running to Garmisch-Partenkirchen from Austria is the route from Innsbruck via the German town of Mittenwald. The only other route from Austria, and a major one at that, is from Innsbruck through Kufstein and connecting near Rosenheim with the Munich to Salzburg railway.

## The Railways

### D1 – Oberstaufen to Immenstadt

The main line, non-electrified, in western Bavaria is from Lindau on Lake Constance (Bodensee) to Munich via Kempten, Kaufbeuren and Buchloe, a total distance of 220 km. Having left Lindau (alt. 398 m), trains start to climb up to Hergatz and then on to Rothenbach (Allgau) before reaching Oberstaufen (alt. 784 m). Oberstaufen (population 7,142) is a tourist centre and health spa, the popularity of which is best illustrated by the fact that there are an amazing 3,500 registered second homes in the town! From here,

Locomotive No. 223070 hauls an Arriva Länderbahn Express (ALEX) towards Oberstaufen on 14th March, 2009. *Author*

A DB Regio service heads for Obertsdorf, here seen passing the village of Fischen on 14th March, 2009.    *Author*

the railway follows the river and the main road, known as the Alpenstraß, for 17 km before dropping down to the town of Immenstadt (population 14,238). The scenery of the mountains to the south, the Hochgrat (1,834 m) and the Stuiben (1,749 m) is excellent. Just before the line reaches Immenstadt trains skirt the northern side of the large and beautiful Allsee lake. The old town of Immenstadt is pedestrianised. Within the town is the 1620-built Königsegg Palace, a most attractive landmark and well worth visiting. Immenstadt is also famous for its Allgäuer cheeses which are celebrated in various festivals throughout the year. In September, the town hosts a special cattle round-up, the only one to be had in Germany. It is a kind of an equivalent to what the French do for sheep – the *transhumance*. In February each year, another festival, the *Funkenfeuer*, is celebrated on the mountains. It is like the UK's bonfire night where, instead of Guy Fawkes, the effigy of a witch is burned. May Day is celebrated here as elsewhere in Bavaria and, for that matter, throughout Germany. Most towns and villages have their tall blue and white May Poles often decorated with the town/village emblems and the shields of the various local workers' guilds. Strict rules govern the May Day celebrations. Many poles are are now permanent fixtures but that was not always the case. Temporary structures used to be erected which needed to be protected from young men from neighbouring villages stealing them before the day. If the 'larceny' should be successful the pole would be returned after negotiations had been concluded over barrels of beer and food!

## D2 – Immenstadt to Obertsdorf

From Immenstadt a single track railway, again non-electrified, heads south for 21 km through Sonthofen to Obertsdorf (alt. 828 m). The railway traces the main road and the River Iller. Mountains to the west of the line are the Stuiben (1,749 m) and the

Riedbergerhorn (1,787 m) and to the east in the Allgäuer Alpen are the Grünten (1,738 m), the Wertachler Hörnle (1,695 m), Nebelhorn (2,224 m) and the Gr Daumen (2,280 m). Sonthofen, with a population of 21,303, is claimed to be the most southerly town in Germany. It is surrounded by mountains, lakes and forests and is a popular tourist destination throughout the year. Adolf Hitler built the 'Ordensburg' here, a place where young boys were trained for later service in the Nazi Party. In World War II, Sonthofen was bombed twice but the Ordensburg building managed to escape destruction. The next village 3 km down the line is Altstädten, again a popular tourist venue. Fischen, a little further on, has some history that it would rather forget. During World War II there was an annex here of the Dachau concentration camp, the main camp being situated 16 km north-west of Munich. The terminus of the line is reached with the final ascent to Obertsdorf, 828 m above sea level. Here again the village is popular for winter sports and is one of the few, if not the only one in Germany, which has an outdoor ice rink open throughout the year. Obertsdorf features in the Four Hills World Cup ski-jumping competition that takes place over four days around each New Year. The tournament hill here is the Schattenbergschanze. The other hills in the competition are the Große Olympiaschanze not far away at Garmisch-Partenkirchen, the Bergiselschanze near Innsbruck and the Paul-Ausserleitner-Schanze at Bischofshofen in Austria. Obertsdorf has the record ski-jump for all of the tournament hills. Sigurd Petterson of Norway, who, in 2003, managed a ski jump of 143.5 m, currently holds the record.

## D3 – Nesselwang to Pfronten-Steinach

The city of Kempten has a direct rail connection with Garmisch-Partenkirchen, part of which travels through Austria's Tyrol via Reutte (*see entry A27*). Nesselwang (alt. 864 m) is the start of the

A DB Regio service approaches the level crossing near Voglen heading for Nesselwang on 14th March, 2009.                    *Author*

Bavarian section of this Alpine railway travelling to the Austrian border at Pfronten-Steinach, a distance of 10 km. Nesselwang is a small town with just over 3,600 inhabitants but throughout the year over 73,000 holiday guests swell the numbers, a strong indicator of its attraction as a tourist resort. In 1429, King Sigismund granted Nesselwang the right to have a market; it continues to this day. It is a most picturesque affair and the target both of the amateur and the more serious photographer. The town, standing at the foot of the Alpspitz (1,575 m) has a lift (Alspitzbahn) which takes skiers almost to the summit. In summer, the lift is equally popular with walkers and mountain bikers accessing the mountains.

### D4 – Griesen to Garmisch-Partenkirchen

The Kempten to Garmisch-Partenkirchen disappears into Austria at Pfronten-St Stainach and passes through Austria for 29 km before re-emerging into Germany at Griesen. The small village of Griesen (alt. 818 m) is at the foot of Germany's highest mountain, the Zugspitze (2,962 m) which has a rack/cogwheel railway to take visitors close to the summit (*see entry D5*). The electrified route to Garmisch-Partenkirchen, 13 km east, runs for most of the way alongside the picturesque Loisach river passing through Untergrainau and Hausbergbahn before reaching Garmisch-Partenkirchen. At Hausbergbahn, it is possible to disembark and hop on to a train on the Zugspitzbahn or take the cable car up the Hausberghöhe (1,347 m). Other mountains, in addition to the Zugspitze, which can be seen from this railway, are the Waxenstein (2,275 m), Osterfelderkopf (2,150 m), the Alpspitze (2,628 m) and the Kreuzeck und Hausberg (1,638 m). The highest peaks in the area run along the Austrian border, where the mountain ridges of the Wettersteingebirge and the Karwendelgebirge rise. The valley, together with the surrounding mountains, is called the Werdenfelser Land. Further north the ridges of the Ammergebirge and the Estergebirge dominate with peaks still in excess of 2,000 m. In the northernmost parts of the district there are the alpine uplands (about 600 m high). Garmisch-Partenkirchen (alt. 708 m) is a large market town (population 26,112) standing on the banks of the River Partnach. The towns of Garmisch and the older Partenkirchen were once separate entities but in 1935 their respective mayors were ordered by Adolf Hitler to combine the towns in anticipation of the 1936 Winter Olympic Games. They complied! Given the proximity of the Zugspitze and its neighbouring mountains, the town is a popular holiday resort all the year round. In addition to the railway, a fast motorway from Munich makes access very easy, even for day trips. The composer Richard Strauss was at one time a resident of Garmisch-Partenkirchen.

### D5 – Zugspitzbahn

The building of the Zugspitzbahn began in 1928 with the final section to Schneefernerhaus on the Zugspitzplatt completed in July 1930. Today Tourismus-Service Zugspitzland operates the Zugspitzbahn all the year round. The total length of the line from Garmisch-Partenkirchen to the summit station on the Zugspitzplatt is 19 km. The service is very popular throughout the year carrying up to 600 persons per hour. Stations or halts on the route are Hausbergbahn, Kreuzeck-Alspitzbahn, Hammersbach-Höllental, Grainau, Ausweiche 1 (en. passing loop), Eibsee, Ausweiche 3, Riffelriss, Ausweiche 4 and Höllental. The line is metre gauge and to climb/descend the mountain a rack/cogwheel system is utilized based on the Riggenbach design. Such a system is vital as the line rises from 710 m to 2,600 m, a height difference of 1,890 m with the steep gradients varying along the route. The gradient on the Garmisch-Partenkirchen and Grainau sections is no more than 3.51 per cent; Grainau and Eibsee it is up to 14 per cent; and, from Eibsee

DB Regio railcar No. 426 028-7 runs alongside the River Loisach heading for Reutte on 21st October, 2007.

*Author*

Zugspitzbahn's rack/cogwheel railcar No. 12 leaves Eibsee for the summit on 21st October, 2007.                                *Author*

to the Zugspitzplatt it reaches 25 per cent. The total journey time is 58 minutes with the non-rack-assisted section between Garmisch-Partenkirchen and Grainau taking just 13 minutes, the rack-assisted sections between Grainau and Eibsee taking 10 minutes and the final and steepest section, also rack-assisted, between Eibsee and the Zugspitzplatt taking 35 minutes. The railcars and locomotives used are electrically-powered at 1650V DC. Those used for the section between Garmisch-Partenkirchen and Grainau are Beh 4/8s double railcars. Thereafter, and to the summit station, single unit rack/cogwheel assisted railcars, Beh 4/4s, are used. These were originally built in 1956 but since updated by Stadler Company. For more information about this railway, see the website www.zugspitzland.de

### D6 – Murnau to Garmisch-Partenkirchen

The double track main line route (electrified) south from Munich travels via Starnberg past the beautiful Starnberger See to Tutzing where the railway bifurcates. The eastern section, single track, becomes the Kochelseebahn (*see entry D10*) and the western spur, also single track, continues down to Murnau and Garmisch-Partenkirchen. Murnau am Staffelsee, to give its full title, is a market town (population 12,086) located close to the Staffelsee lake to its west. Murnau is a minor railway hub with trains leaving there for Oberammergau (*see next entry*). Murnau has a claim to fame for railway enthusiasts in that it was here that Germany's first electrically-operated signal box was installed. Murnau was founded in the late 12th century but suffered a catastrophic fire in 1835 that led to most of the town needing to be completely re-built. At the beginning of World War II a Prisoner of War camp for Polish military officers was established here known as Oflag VII-A Murnau. Initially, it housed 1,000 officers including one Rear Admiral, four Divisional Generals and 26 Brigadier Generals. By 1945, the camp had a prisoner population of over 5,000. The Rear

A DB service 'tailed' by electric locomotive No. 111 036-0 arrives at Oberau station bound for Munich on 13th March, 2009.    *Author*

Admiral was Józef Michal Hubert Unrug (1884-1973), a German-born Pole who helped the re-building of the Polish Navy after World War I. In 1925 he became its overall commander. When Germany invaded Poland in 1939, Unrug executed a plan, 'Operation Peking', for the strategic withdrawal of the Polish Navy's major vessels to the United Kingdom. That done and with no Navy left to command, Unrug became commander of Poland's land forces. His priority was to prevent Germany's recovery of the Polish Corridor. However, after Warsaw and Modlin fell, he felt continued resistance was futile and so, on 2nd October, 1939, he and his troops capitulated. He spent the rest of the war in various prison camps, including Colditz, before coming to Murnau where he was the most senior-ranking officer and commander of the Polish soldiers interned there. He was treated with great respect as a former German officer by the Germans. They brought many former Imperial German Navy colleagues to visit him with the intention of encouraging him to switch sides. Unrug responded by refusing to speak German, pretending that he had forgotten the language in September 1939. Much to the irritation of the Germans he would always insist on having a interpreter present! Unrug's spirit and unbending attitude was an inspiration to his fellow prisoners.

## D7 – Murnau to Oberammergau

Oberammergau is a large village of 5,364 souls. It is situated at the foot of the Hochshergen (1,396 m), Teufelstättkopf and Laubeneck (1,759 m), Notkarspitze (1,889 m) and the distinctive Matterhorn-shaped Kofel (1,342 m) mountains in the Garmisch-Partenkirchen district of Upper Bavaria. As with many villages in the Bavarian Alps, it is popular throughout the year for its outdoor pursuits, its history and its picturesque painted houses. Many of these houses are decorated with *Lüftlmalerei* (frescoes) depicting fairy tales, religious scenes and Bavarian themes. Woodcarving is a local speciality and there are shops selling such pieces which are especially popular at Christmas. Oberammergau is also well known for its NATO school (an Operational Training and Education facility) which has been established there since 1953. However, the village's greatest claim to worldwide fame is for its performances every decade of the Passion Play. In 1663, the village suffered from the Great Plague and many lives were lost. In response, the villagers collectively made a solemn vow that, if further lives were spared, the whole village would enact a play depicting the story of Christ's suffering, dying and resurrection. The Plague did not claim any more lives and so the following year the villagers, in gratitude, enacted their first play. They have continued to do so every decade since in spite of wars and other problems. The performances are delivered in years ending in a zero, the only exception being in 1984 for the 350th anniversary. In 2010, the village will enact the play for the 41st time, performances running throughout May to October. The event involves over 2,000 actors, singers, instrumentalists and technicians, all residents of the village. Accessing Oberammergau by train is from Murnau on a single track electrified line via Saulgrub which, at 859 m, is the highest point on the line. The distance covered is almost 24 km.

## D8 – König Ludwigbahn

Construction of the railway from Marktoberdorf to Füssen, a distance of 31 km, began in the early 1870s with the final section to Füssen opened in June 1889. In its earliest days it was operated by the Royal Bavarian State Railways (K.Bay.Sts.B) which, at its height between 1844 and the end of World War I, had an 8,526 km network in southern Germany. In October 1933, the K.Bay.Sts.B was nationalized and became part of the Reichsbahn. The route has never been electrified. The route is a secondary line off the Lindau

On the Murnau to Oberammergau route a DB Regio railcar set is photographed near Grafenaschau on 13th March, 2009. *Author*

A DB passenger service from Füssen towards Marktoberdorf photographed between Reinertshof and Weizern-Hopferau on 14th March, 2009.
*Author*

Germany meets Austria at Scharnitz station in Austria on 28th June, 2007. *Author*

to Munich main line at Bissenhoffen from where it travels 6½ km down to Marktoberdorf. Apart from Füssen, this is the only main town on the route. Marktoberdorf (population 18,339) is a medium-sized town and capital of the Bavarian Ostallgäu district. It is well known to certain international computer scientists for it is here, since 1970, that a NATO inspired two-week summer school has been convened. The end of the line is Füssen on the River Lech which flows into the nearby Forggensee lake. It lies 5 km from the Austrian border which can be accessed by a mountain road. The town is the highest in Bavaria (808 m). Its outstanding landmark, standing high above the town, is the Hohes Schloss, the former summer residence of the Bishop Princes of Augsburg and is one of the largest and best-preserved late Gothic castles. Located nearby are the huge tourist attractions of the Neuschwanstein and Hohenschwangau castles. The Neuschwanstein (en. New Swan Palace) is a 19th century construction sited on a hill between Hohenschwangau and Füssen. The palace was commissioned by the eccentric King Ludwig II of Bavaria (1845-1886) as a personal retreat and in homage to the composer Richard Wagner, sponsored by, and a favourite of the king. The fairy-tale castle (almost Disney-like) is one of the most photographed buildings in Germany. Also near Füssen and the German village of Schwangau is the Hohenschwangau Castle (en. Castle of the High Swan County), again a 19th century castle built between 1833 and 1837 by Ludwig's father, King Maximilian II of Bavaria. In an annex to the castle was the childhood residence of Ludwig and his brother, later King Otto I of Bavaria. The railway takes its name from Ludwig, who was also known as the Fairy Tale King or Swan King. He was an interesting, indeed eccentric character and although he only lived 40 years he left an indelible mark on German history. Ludwig, sometimes unkindly referred to as 'Mad King Ludwig', was removed from his throne on 12th June, 1886 on the grounds of alleged paranoia; he was succeeded by his uncle Luitpold, acting as

Regent. The following evening, after he had been deposed, Ludwig together with one of the certifying psychiatrists, Dr Bernhard von Gudden, went for a walk on the shores of Lake Starnberg. At 23.30 hours the two were found dead by the lake. The much-questioned verdict, then and since, was suicide by drowning.

### D9 – Mittenwaldbahn

This route, overall 60 kilometres in length, connects Garmisch-Partenkirchen with Innsbruck via the small town of Mittenwald, hence the name given to the railway. The line, single track and electrified, heads east from Garmish-Partenkirchen to Klais (the highest main line station in Germany) from where it heads south to Mittenwald, last station in Germany, before heading down to Scharnitz station with its distinctive light green decor, the first station in Austria. The Mittenwaldbahn, now with a name change to Karwendelbahn (*see entry A26*), continues south to Innsbruck, capital of the Tyrol. The journey between Garmish-Partenkirchen and Scharnitz runs for half of the route alongside the attractive Isar river. The journey takes about 40 minutes on services provided on a shared basis by Germany's DB or Austria's ÖBB. Mittenwald (population *circa* 3,000) is a popular tourist resort given the attraction of the local mountain, the Karwendelspitze (2,385 m) which dominates the town. A cable car rising to an altitude of 2,244 m provides easy access to the summit. On the other side of town are the foothills of the Wetterstein popular in summer with walkers and in winter where the foothills have been transformed into the principal downhill ski area of the Kranzberg. The town is also world famous for the manufacture of stringed instruments, specifically violins, violas and cellos. There is a museum here dedicated to the manufacture of the violin and to Matthias Klotz (1653-1743), the founder of this local industry.

The Kochelseebahn on 13th March, 2009 with a DB service seen near the hamlet of Ort heading for Kochel 2 km further down the line.
*Author*

**D10 – Kochelseebahn**

This route is between Tutzing and Kochel, a distance of 36 km. Tutzing is a small town (population 9,427) 12 km south of Starnberg and on the western shores of the Starnberger See where King Ludwig II allegedly drowned in Bavaria (*see entry D8*). The town recently gained international notoriety by becoming the centre of a heated debate on Germany's former National Socialism (Nazi). An Honorary Citizen of Tutzing is the late Elly Ney (1882-1968) a pianist, an active Nazi and a Hitler-devotee. In 2008, Tutzing's then new mayor, executed his rights as 'landlord' of the Town Hall and took down a portrait of Ney that hung there. It unleashed a huge debate - the *causa Ney*. Questions were posed as to whether Ney should also be stripped of her honorary citizenship. Countless German press articles, several academics, the president of the German Jewish Federation and many Tutzing citizens all voiced their views. It was said that her continuing honorary status, as well as the debate itself, was shameful and embarrassing to modern Germany and to the town itself. Despite the strong support for her removal as an honorary citizen, and also to rename the street carrying her name, Tutzing's (ultra conservative) community council decided, in January 2009, to maintain the status quo. Tutzing is where the railway from Munich bifurcates with the western section travelling down to Weilhem and Murnau (*see entry D6*). The eastern section, an electrified single track line, travels 35 km to Kochel at the northern end of the Kochelsee and Walchensee, yet more lakes with popular tourist appeal. Kochel am See (to give it its full title) has a total of 4,400 inhabitants but this number is multiplied many-fold throughout the year by a visiting population. Fourteen kilometres further south, is the Walchensee Power Plant, a high pressure power station delivering a whopping output of 124 megawatts, and one of the largest of its kind in Germany. It was here, in 1943, that a wind tunnel was delivered for the development of the V2 rocket. After the end of World War II, the wind tunnel was moved to White Oak, Maryland (USA) where rocket studies were continued. Kochel is renowned for the myth of 'The Smith of Kochel' a local Bavarian farmer who allegedly led a rebellion against Austro-Hungarian occupation. He is said to have performed many heroic deeds. Historical research suggests the story is purely one of legend but try telling that to the locals! Whilst the railway ends here, the main road continues over the border to Innsbruck.

**D11 – Holzkirchen to Lenggries and Tegernsee**

Bayerische Oberland-Bahn GmbH (BOB) part of Veolia Transport, is the concession, founded in 1998, which operates the exclusively diesel-operated services from Munich via Holzkirchen to Lenggries and Tegernsee. It also operates services to Bayerischzell (*see next entry*). The total network amounts to 120 km on which 21 rail vehicles are operated, made up mainly of 'Integral' but also three 'Talent' railcars built by Bombardier Talbot. Whilst trains run to and from Munich, Holzkirchen is where BOB comes into its own. There are two services delivered from here to Lenggries, a distance of 66 km via Schaftlach; and, from the latter, to Tegernsee a distance of 12.3 km. Holzkirchen is a town of 16,050 inhabitants. Its main claim to international fame is that it was from here that Radio Free Europe operated its transmissions to Eastern Bloc countries between 1951 and 2004. It is said that the electromagnetic forces put out by the powerful transmitters (250kW) caused a Tornado aircraft to crash not far away near Oberlaindern in the 1980s. Eleven kilometres down the line is Schaftlach where the line branches off to Tegernsee. However, the main line continues from there to Bad Tolz (population 17,648) a small market town on the banks of the Isar river and standing at an altitude of 670 m. The town suffered a bad fire in 1453 exacerbated by most of the buildings being constructed in wood; the town was re-built but this time mainly in stone! Wood and salt were for

A BOB diesel unit No. VT 112 comes from Bayerischzell heading for Schliersee on 12th March, 2009. Wendelstein provides the background.                                                                                        *Author*

centuries the local products but in the 19th century natural springs were found locally and the town became a popular spa. Tolz, which became Bad Tolz in 1899, is known for its spectacular views of the Alps to the south. Lenggries (population 9,553) 9 km further on and the terminus of the line, enjoys similar views. This town stands at an altitude of 700 m and has to the east the Tegernsee mountains and to the west the Brauneck mountain (1,555 m). The Brauneck and its environs are a well-known ski area which contribute to the local economy which is centred almost exclusively on tourism. Back up the line to Schaftlach, as already mentioned, the branch line diverts to Tegernsee. The line is 12.3 km long and from Gmund travels for almost 5 km alongside the beautiful lake of Tegernsee. The town (population 5,000) is dominated by the Hirschberg mountain (1,668 m) and is very popular with tourists. The English 19th century historian Lord Acton died here in 1902; two of his famous quotations are 'Power tends to corrupt; absolute power corrupts absolutely. Great men are almost always bad men' and 'Liberty is not the power of doing what we like, but the right to do what we ought'. For more information about the railway, see www.bayerische-oberlandbahn.de

### D12 – Holzkirchen to Bayrischzell

Another service operated by Bayerische Oberland-Bahn GmbH (BOB) is the route from Munich via Holzkirchen to Bayrischzell. The line for the 24.6 km from Holzkirchen to Schliersee is double track. From there, and for a further 16.7 km, it is single track to Bayrischzell. In common with all BOB-operated lines it is not electrified. The view from a train window is picturesque all of the way but becomes more dramatic as Schliersee is reached. Schliersee is a well-known holiday, health and winter sports centre with a regular population of about 6,500 inhabitants. It lies in the Miesbacher Oberland, the so-called 'soul of Bavaria'. The large lake

of Schliersee is an obvious major attraction but so are the Spitzingsee mountain lakes which are considered to hold water of the highest quality. The highest mountain in the Spitzingsee area is the Croda Rossa (1,884 m). Given the proximity of Munich to this area with excellent rail and road communications, the traveller is warned that the area is very busy all the year round, especially at weekends. Beyond Schliersee is Fischhausen Neuhaus where the railway turns east. Ahead is the magnificent Wendelstein (*see next entry*) and to the right (south) are the Wallberg (1,722 m), Rotwand (1,885 m), Hinteres Sonmwendjoch (1,985 m) and the Brünnstein (1,619 m) mountains of the Mangfallgebirge. The penultimate stop before reaching the terminus at Bayrischzell, is Osterhofen from where the Wendelstein cable car operates. Bayrischzell (alt. 804 m) has a resident population of 1,584 but at any time of the year this is well supplemented by visitors staying in the many local hotels, hostels and b&bs. Winter skiing is an obvious attraction but snowboarding and cross-country skiing are equally popular. Athletic pursuits do not stop when the snow melts. Nordic walking has become very popular locally and is encouraged specifically in May each year with the 'Nordic Walk Oberland', a challenging event held over a 21 km course.

### D13 – Wendelsteinbahn

The Wendelstein mountain (1,838 m) near the townships of Brannenburg and Kufstein, is a popular venue with ramblers all the year round who are aided by the regular cable car and rack/cogwheel railway services. The cable car facility was built in 1969 and operates from the valley station (alt. 792 m) at Bayrischzell Osterhofen found on the southern side of the mountain. The summit station is located at an altitude of 1,724 m and the journey in the 50-person cabin-car takes seven minutes to ascend the 2.95 km journey with a maximum gradient of 58 per

A BOB service No. VT 113 passes the Tegernsee on 12th March, 2009.

*Author*

Wendelsteinbahn's Beh 4/8 12 approaches the terminus at Brannenburg on 12th March, 2009. *Author*

The 'Wachtl Express' on 26th June, 2006.

*Courtesy of Kiefersfelden Community Council*

cent. The views on the way up on the all-to-short a journey are fantastic. However, on reaching the summit station all is not over as it is possible to walk, in about 20 minutes, to a viewpoint near the summit called the Gacher Blick (en. steep view). From there, the traveller can appreciate the 360° panoramic views of the Wilder Kaiser and the majestic peaks of the Wetterstein, Rofan and Karwendel mountain ranges. Near the summit on a small side peak, the Schwaigerwand, is the Kircherl, a small Bavarian Chapel built in 1889. It is claimed to be Germany's highest consecrated church where it is still possible to get married. Also located near the summit is the Wendelstein House where one can enjoy a meal. On the actual summit which takes about an hour to reach from the cable car/cog railway is a meteorological station and observatory. It is open to visitors on the first Thursday of each month between May and September. Also of interest is a cave network which criss-crosses beneath the peak. The other means of ascent and prime focus of this entry is by the Wendelstein rack/cogwheel railway. Between 1910 and 1912, Otto von Steinbeis constructed the almost 10 km-long railway line employing 800 workers mainly of Bosnian origin. They built seven tunnels, eight galleries and 12 bridges but the greatest challenges (and costs) were the retaining walls for the trackbed. The actual route of the railway is 7.66 km in length. The track leaves the station near Brannenburg (alt. 508 m) and rises on a maximum gradient of 23.7 per cent to the summit station standing at an altitude of 1,724 m. The gauge is a metre wide and 6½ km of the route is aided by a rack/cogwheel system designed by Emil Strub. This system, its benefit being it is the easiest of all rack/cogwheel systems to maintain, is also utilised on the Jungfraubahn in Switzerland (*see entry CH18*). The electricity supply operating at 1500V DC is delivered by overhead catenary. The modern railcars, which are now used, carry a maximum 200 passengers and take 30 minutes to achieve the ascent. To make for a full and enjoyable day out many visitors make a complete tour,

what is referred to locally as the 'ring line'. This involves going up on the cog railway, down in the cable car and back to the departure point by frequently running buses (see www.wendelstein-ringlinie.de) For more information about this excellent railway, see www.wendelsteinbahn.de/bergbahnen/international/englisch.php

**D14 – Wachtl Express**

At Kiefersfelden, 85 km north-east of Innsbruck and right on the border with Austria's Tyrol region, is the Rohrdorfer Zement enterprise which is part of the Heidelberg Cement Group. Here, the company operates two Krokodil-type electric-powered locomotives built in 1929 and 1930. For excursions, they each haul three 1912-constructed passenger carriages previously obtained from the nearby Wendelsteinbahn (*see previous entry*). However, passenger traffic is not this company's main business, indeed far from it. The line on which this service operates is an industrial railway used daily with between 12 and 14 journeys transporting quarried limestone to the Kiefersfelden works for the production of cement. The 5 km route is on narrow gauge track (900 mm) and goes from the aforementioned Kiefersfelden to Thiersee-Wachtl, the latter actually being in Austria, thus making this line truly international! The journey takes 20 minutes. The service came about as a joint initiative, taken in 1990, by the Kiefersfelden Municipality with Rohrdorfer Zement to operate an occasional tourist service on the line in the summer. Each year, eight weekends are selected between late June and early October to run the two return services on Saturdays and three on Sundays. More information about the tourist service, known locally as 'Nostalgie-Express Wachtlbahn' can be obtained from www.kiefersfelden.de/freizeit/wachtl.php

### D15 – Prien am See to Aschau

East of Rosenheim, on the main Munich-Rosenheim-Salzburg line (*see entry D19*) is Bad Endorf. From here, tourist trains are operated on the Chiemgauer Lokalbahn running 'oldtimer' railcars for the 45 minute, 18.5 km journey to and from Obing. Services operate on Sundays and public holidays between early May and early October. More detail is not provided here because the railway falls outside the definition of 'alpine'. However, more information can be obtained from the website www.chiemgauer-lokalbahn.de Travelling a further 7 km east from Bad Endorf, the town of Prien is reached. From here the Chiemseebahn operates a steam tramway, said to be the oldest continuously running in the world, over a short length (1.7 km) of metre gauge track to Stock on the shores of the massive lake of Chiemsee (visit www.chiemsee-schifffahrt.de). The route, which is the focus of this entry, however, is from Prien am See south to Aschau. This is a short single track non-electrified line travelling a total distance of 9.6 km through the villages of Urschalling, Vachendorf, Umrathshausen and Ort following the Prien river for much of the way. Prien is a convenient location for touring the lake and the mountains which form the backdrop. At the other end of the line is the pretty village of Aschau with its huge castle (de. *Schloss*) dominating the village. The village stands at the foot of the Kampenwand (1,668 m) on which a cable car service operates. There is a local Birds of Prey Centre that gives displays every day except Mondays from May to October. It is a fantastic sight to see eagles, buzzards and hawks fly in the context of their natural mountainous terrain.

A DB service from Prien to Aschau on 13th March, 2009.

*Author*

## D16 – Traunstein to Ruhpolding

Continuing the journey on the main line towards Salzburg the traveller reaches Traunstein (population 18,351) 11 km east of the Chiemsee. To the south, 15 km away are the Alps and 30 km further east is Salzburg. Perhaps the town's most famous inhabitant for a time was Joseph Alois Ratzinger (1927- ) who attended the local Seminary before moving to Munich for his university studies. He was born in Bavaria (Marktl am Inn) and in April 2005 became the 265th Pope – Benedict XVI. From Traunstein there are three branch lines operating. To the north-north-west is a single track non-electrified line travelling 13 km to Hörpolding from where there is a short industrial line leading to a Siemens factory. Beyond Hörpolding, the line continues to Mühldorf. The second branch line, 10 km long, runs from Hufschlag just east of Traunstein up to Waging am See (population 6,000) close to the Waginger See. There is the 'Bajuwarenmuseum' here which records the history of the ancient Bavarians. The third branch line from Traunstein run south into the mountains and to Ruhpolding (population 6,319). Ruhpolding is a popular destination for sportsmen and women as well as tourists all the year round. It houses a famous biathlon track. (NB: Biathlon is a combination of the sports of cross-country skiing with rifle-shooting.) Ruhpolding was the centre for the Biathlon World Championships in 1979, 1985 and 1996. In 2007, the World Championship Mountain Bike 24 hour Race was also hosted here. The railway is an electrified single track, 13 km in length, and traces the Traun river as it heads towards its source beyond Ruhpolding on the Durrnbachhorn (1,775 m) mountain. At one time a narrow (metre) gauge used to continue from Ruhpolding for 22½ km into the mountains passing the lakes of the Mittersee and Weitsee before reaching the winter sports village of Reit in Winkl. The railway was closed in the 1930s following some accidents coupled with the high costs of maintaining the line. The trackbed is now used for cycling in summer and nordic skiing in winter. When it was operating, travelling on this railway must have been a fantastic experience.

## D17 – Freilassing to Berchtesgaden

Very close to the German/Austrian border and the City of Salzburg is Freilassing (population 16,000) which can trace its past to Neolithic times. It was settled by Celts and later Romans. Until 1923 it was known as Salzburghofen. It became an important railway centre dominating the local economy for a long time. Very little of the old town now exists. Given its proximity to Hitler's Eagle's Nest, it was popular stopping off point for top Nazis *en route* there. It also housed a Wehrmacht (German Army) depot making it an important strategic target for Allied bombing. In April 1945, a matter of days before the end of World War II, Freilassing was almost completely destroyed. The railway from Freilassing is electrified and double track for its 14.9 km following all the way the River Saalach to Bad Reichenhall. From there, still electrified, the railway is single track for its final 18.8 km to Berchtesgaden. Bad Reichenhall, with a population of 18,351, is a spa town and the administrative capital of the Berchtesgadener Land. It is encircled by the Chiemgauer Alps, including Mount Staufen (1,771 m) and Mount Zwiesel (1,781 m). Bad Reichenhall has traditionally been a centre for the production of salt which is evaporated from local brine ponds. Like Freilassing, Bad Reichenhall experienced heavy bombing in April 1945; over 200 people lost their lives. The town also suffered a terrible accident in 2006 when the roof of the Ice Rink collapsed killing 15 people, 12 of them children, and injuring 34 others. At Berchtesgaden (population 7,752) stood the Berchtesgadener Hof Hotel until it was demolished in 2006. At various times it hosted Eva Braun, Erwin Rommel, Josef Goebbels and Heinrich Himmler as well as Neville Chamberlain and David Lloyd George. The Berchtesgaden area, a National Park since 1978, is often linked by mountaineers with the Mount Watzmann (2,713 m) the third-highest mountain in Germany after the Zugspitze and the Hochwanner. It is revered by rock climbers for its *Ostwand* (en. east face). To the south of the village is the deepest lake in Germany,

DB double diesel railcar No. 426 029-5 runs alongside the River Traun near Siegsdorf towards Traunstein on 11th March, 2009.

*Author*

A Linie Salzburg service in heavy snow crosses the River Saalach near to Bad Reichenhall on 11th March, 2009. *Author*

An ÖBB 'Railjet' No. 1016 034-9 heads a passenger service for Salzburg on 11th March, 2009. *Author*

the Königssee. Another notable, or perhaps notorious, mountain peak, is the Kehlstein (1,834 m) on which there is the *Kehlsteinhaus* (en. Eagle's Nest). From its perch, the Eagle's Nest enjoys breathtaking views over Berchtesgaden and the surrounding areas. Commissioned by Martin Bormann it took just 13 months to build including the construction of a difficult 6.5 km road from Obersalzberg to the house. Contrary to popular belief it was not used much by Hitler, he only visited it perhaps 10 times and usually for no more than 30 minutes. The building was probably saved from destruction after World War II because of the lack of close association with Hitler.

## D18 – Kufstein to Rosenheim

The railway between the two Austrian cities of Innsbruck and Salzburg is an important international rail corridor. It can be divided into two sections, viz: Kufstein to Rosenheim and Rosenheim to Salzburg (*see next entry*). From Innsbruck the railway travels north-east through Jenbach (home to the Achenseebahn – *see entry A22*) and Wörgl before reaching Kufstein Grenze, the Austrian-German border. Just over the border is Kiefersfelden from where the Wachtl Express operates (*see entry D14*). The line to Rosenheim is just under 32 km long passing Brannenburg, from where the Wendelsteinbahn operates (*see entry D13*) and Raubling. The valley, through which the railway runs, belongs to the River Inn which can be observed for much of the journey. On either side are mountains, notably to the west the Brünnstein (1,619 m) and the Wendelstein (1,837 m) and to the east the Pyramidenspitze (1,997 m) and other mountains of the Chiemgauer. Operating on this route are the Austrian Railways (ÖBB) new Railjet services running between Austria, Germany and Hungary. They began services in 2008 and offer state-of-the-art transport offering maximum comfort, contemporary design and high level of service, the watchwords of Railjet. Three classes of travel are offered – Economy, First and Premium. The Taurus classes of locomotives, 1016, 1116 and 1216, built by Siemens haul the trains. The train sets, in addition to the locomotive, are comprised of a driving trailer and six intermediate carriages offering 408 seats. Overall, the trains are up to 205 m in length and are capable of running at speeds of 230 kmh.

## D19 – Rosenheim to Salzburg

The second section of the international route is from Rosenheim where rail traffic comes in from Munich, 52 km to the north-west. The railway from Munich to Salzburg was originally named the Maximilianstraß in honour of the then King of Bavaria, father of King Ludwig II. Rosenheim, a town with a population of 60,000 and as many again living in the greater conurbation, is a central location in this region and has for centuries been an important staging post. The first railway station in the town was built in 1858 and operated for only 18 years but as rail traffic grew it quickly became too small. However, the original building survived and is now the Town Hall (de. *Rathaus*). Rosenheim station is the largest station between Munich, Innsbruck and Salzburg and is always very busy, day and night. This is despite the fact that since the 1980s through trains have by-passed the main station to the south by taking the Rosenheim curve (de. *Rosenheimer kurve*). The route to Salzburg totals 88.6 km of double track electrified line passing alongside the Simmsee, through Bad Endorf, Prien am See, by the Chiemsee, through Traunstein and Freilassing. Incidentally, near to the railway station in Freilassing town (address: Westendstraße, 5) is the 'Eisenbahnmuseum Lokwelt Freilassing'. This railway museum, with a most interesting collection, is open every day (1000-1700 hours) all the year round except on 1st November, 24th/25th December and 1st January. It is well worth a visit. For more information, see the website: www.lokwelt.freilassing.de

A DB service led by a Taurus class '1116' (out of shot) between Rosenheim and Bernau on 11th March, 2009.  *Author*

# Switzerland

## Introduction

Switzerland, perhaps more so than any of its neighbours, is the one most associated in people's minds with the Alps. Switzerland is a landlocked country in Western Europe. It has a population of about 7.7 million people and geographically is small with an area of 41,285 sq. km (15,940 sq. miles). Comprising 26 states or cantons, Switzerland is governed as a federal republic. Berne (population 128,000) is the capital and home of the federal government. Other important cities are Geneva, Basel and Zürich. Switzerland is one of the richest countries in the world and Zug is its richest canton.

Most of the southern and centrally located cantons of Switzerland administer some part of Switzerland's Alps. Notable for a high concentration of peaks are three running in the south along the French, Italian and Austrian borders, i.e. Graubünden, Ticino and Valais.

France borders Switzerland to the west, Italy to the south, Austria and Liechtenstein to the east and Germany to the north. Switzerland is a neutral country and is not a member of the European Union. The country is multilingual having four national languages, French, Italian, German, and Romansh which is spoken by 35,000 residents mainly in the canton of Graubünden.

Switzerland consists of three geographical areas - the Alps themselves, a central plateau, and, along the north-west border with France, the Jura Mountains. The latter, incidentally, do not fall within the definition of 'Alps' for the purpose of this book. The Swiss Alps mainly comprise the Middle Alps - the high mountain range running across the centre and south of the country. About 60 per cent of the country's geographical area is alpine. Perhaps the most famous mountain is the Matterhorn (4,478 m) in the Pennine Alps but it is not Switzerland's highest mountain, that honour is bestowed upon the Dufourspitze (4,634 m) in the Monte Rosa Massif, which is also the home to other high mountains such as the Dom (4,545 m) and the Weisshorn (4,505 m). Another range, the Bernese Alps, is well known for the Jungfrau (4,158 m), Mönch (4,099 m) and Eiger (3,970 m)

mountains. In the south-east of the country is the Engadin Valley where the world famous resort of St Moritz can be found. Its highest peak is the Piz Bernina (4,049 m) in the Bernina Alps.

Important European rivers trace their sources to Switzerland, i.e. the Rhine, Rhône, Inn, Aare and Ticino. The country is also a land of lakes, viz. Lake Geneva shared with France where it is known as Lac Léman, Lake Zürich, Lake Neuchâtel (the largest in Switzerland) and Lake Constance shared with Germany and also known as the Bodensee.

Road routes into Switzerland's Alps are from France and Italy. In France a high road travels from Chamonix to Martigny via Le Châtelard; a second access is along the southern shores of Lake Geneva from Evian-les-Bains to St Gingolph; and, a third, comparatively minor route, from Abondance to Monthey. Travellers from Italy can enter Switzerland by way of two passes. First, the Gran St Bernardo pass from Aosta and Brig, and, second, from Domodossola via the Simplon Pass. Roads travel each side of Lake Maggiore, i.e. to Locarno from Verbania and to Bellinzona from Como. Another pass, the Splügen, goes from Chiavenna to Thusis. Chiavenna is also the departure point for St Moritz through Soglio. St Moritz is also reached from Tirano via the Bernina Pass.

There are six, perhaps seven international rail routes into Switzerland. The prime route from France is on the Mont Blanc Express from St Gervais-les-Bains to Martigny. There is the possibility, one day, of resurrecting a second access from France (Evian-les-Bains) to St Gingolph along the shores of Lake Geneva. Italy enjoys the facilities of the 19.8 m-long Simplon tunnel from Domodossola to Brig and Domodossola also accesses Bellinzona, famous for its three medieval castles, via Locarno. Along the shores of Lake Maggiore, Luino links to Cadenazzo and further east, near Lake Como, the town of Como links to Lugano (where nearby Agra claims to be the sunniest place in Switzerland). Another rail route is along the western shores of Lake Lugano to Ponte Tresa. Finally, St Moritz is reached from Colico via Tirano.

The steepest funicular in the world heading towards the Emosson Barrage on 30th August, 2008. *Author*

## The Railways

### CH1 – Mont Blanc Express

In the canton of Valais is the town of Martigny (population 14,973), at an altitude of 467 m, lying at a crossroads between Switzerland, France and Italy. One road links the town with Aosta in Italy over the Gran St Bernardo Pass (alt. 2,469 m); and, the other over the Col de la Forclaz (alt. 1,527 m) to Chamonix in France. The town of Martigny, in the 1st century BC, was called Octodorus and was occupied by the Romans notably Servius Sulpicius Galba. He was sent by Julius Caesar with an army to open up for safe passage the Gran St Bernardo Pass. Incidentally, Servius did not remain loyal for he later joined Brutus and Cassius in the assassination of Caesar, for which he subsequently paid the ultimate price. Evidence of Roman occupation is still apparent with an amphitheatre renovated in 1978 and which is now used, amongst other things, for cow (rather than bull!) fights in the early autumn. At Martigny, as well as the remnants of its amphitheatre, there is nearby the Pierre Gianadda Foundation, a world-renowned art gallery and museum, the large size of which is completely disproportionate to the town. The Mont Blanc Express is a shared enterprise with the French (*see entry F18*). Four years before the Martigny-Orsières railway (*see entry CH3*) was built, in 1910, the rail link between Martigny and Le Châtelard had been opened. There had been many requests over the previous 15 years to the Swiss Federal authorities for permission to build the railway but there was much debate about the most appropriate route to take. Eventually, in 1900, approval was granted for the construction of the Martigny-Vernayaz-Salvan-Finhaut-Le Châtelard route. The 'Martigny-Châtelard, Ligne du Valais à Chamonix' Railway Company was formed and work commenced in November 1902. It was completed four years later. Leaving Martigny, the Mont Blanc Express climbs to a maximum height of 2,480 m at Salvan. It was here that Marconi successfully first tested his wireless telegraphy. Shortly after this point, the train arrives at Marécottes, renowned for its alpine zoo. On the train goes to Trétien, passing through the gorge of the Triège where passengers can look down on a staggering drop of 426 m (1,400 ft) to the valley floor. Arriving at Le Châtelard it is possible to alight and take the funicular to the Emosson Barrage (*see next entry*). For a picture of the Mont Blanc Express see entry F18 on page 32.

### CH2 – Emosson Barrage

Located at Le Châtelard, 23 km from Martigny and 19 km from Chamonix, is an attraction park first opened in 1973. Here is reportedly the steepest funicular (87 per cent) in the world. It was constructed in 1920. In a little over 10 minutes, the funicular raises the traveller almost 692 m to an altitude of 1,821 m. From there, a small scenic train usually hauled by a Decauville-type locomotive, powered by accumulators and running on 600 mm track, conveys the traveller to another small funicular called the 'minifunic'. Rising a further 140 m in height, the minifunic links the train terminal with the Emosson Lake station which stands about 30 m above the dam. Originally, there was no minifunic so visitors had to negotiate a steep path to reach the dam (alt. 1,831 m). However, this tended to put people off so, in 1977, a Monorail Cog Railway was constructed. This operated for 11 years during which time it carried over 170,000 passengers. However, operating at an altitude of over 2,000 m for such a prolonged period, brought its reliability into question. In response, in 1991, it was decided to construct the minifunic. The accumulator-driven locomotives are not the only form of transport on the mountain railway. Thanks to the 'Le Châtelard Association of Steam Trains Admirers', steam locomotives are run on the railway for special occasions as well as chartered events. Steam services are also operated on the third weekend each in the months of June, July, August and September. Whichever mode of transport is used to reach the dam, visitors over the 45-minute journey can enjoy the outstanding views of

Mont Blanc and the surrounding areas. The attraction park is open from about late May to mid-October each year. For more information, see the website www.emosson-trains.ch

### CH3 – St Bernard Express (south to Orsières)

The St Bernard Express offers two destinations from the town of Martigny. The first is to Orsières and the second to Le Châble (*see next entry*). Martigny is located on the main line between Lausanne and Brig where most passenger trains stop. From here it is possible to take one of the St Bernard Express services offered by Transports de Martigny et Régions SA (TMRSA). The train leaves Martigny (alt. 467 m) and passes through Martigny Croix and Bovernier before reaching, 13 km on from Martigny, the village of Sembrancher (alt. 717 m). It is here that passengers alight and take a train waiting on an adjacent platform to continue the journey to Orsières. Meanwhile, the original train continues the journey to Le Châble. The train for Orsières continues up the the Val d'Entremont and after 6.2 km on a 3.5 per cent gradient reaches Orsières (alt. 902 m). The large village of Orsières (population 2,736) is in the Val Ferret and stands on the La Dranse de Ferret river and at the foot of four notable mountains, i.e. Le Catogne (2,598 m), La Breya (2,194 m), Le Chatelet (2,537 m) and Six Blanc (2,445 m). From the village its is possible, in winter, to take a 16 km bus journey as far as Champex Lac near to the Saleina glacier. Alternatively, visitors can choose to travel to La Fouly at the foot of Mont Dolent (3,820 m) in the Graain Alps. It is on this mountain that the frontiers of Switzerland, France and Italy meet. In summer, after the snows have melted, a bus service is able to reach the hospice, founded in 1049, on the Gran St Bernardo Pass (2,469 m). Here, a visit can be made to the legendary kennels of the world-famous rescue dogs. The St Bernard dog, 'Barry', was one of the greatest rescue dogs the world has ever seen; in the early part of the 19th century he lived for 14 years and, during his career, saved over 40 lives.

St Bernard Express bound for Orsières standing at Sembrancher station on 30th August, 2008. *Author*

## CH4 – St Bernard Express (east to Le Châble)

The train, which brought passengers from Martigny to Sembrancher, continues to Le Châble (alt. 820 m) in the valley of Bagnes. There is no need for passengers to transfer trains. Leaving Sembrancher (population 796) the train first travels over a magnificent, recently constructed, low viaduct beneath south facing slopes crammed with vines. The train passes through the small village of Etiez and after 6 km reaches Le Châble, a village in the Bagnes Municipality (population 6,538). This large village sits on the banks of the La Dranse de Bagnes river, which flows from the Lac de Mauvoisin located between the mountains of La Ruinette (3,875 m) and the Tournelon Blanc (3,702 m). From Le Châble, there is access to the world famous ski-station of Verbier, which is situated some 600 m above the village at an altitude of 1,500 m. Access is also possible to Bruson, on the opposite side of the valley, which offers smaller, quieter ski slopes. Mountains immediately surrounding Le Châble are Pierre Avoi (2,473 m), Mont Gond (2,667 m) to the north, Bec de Rosses (3,223 m) to the east and Mont Rogneux (3,084 m) to the south. Verbier is part of the 'Four Valleys' ski area, which includes the resorts of Verbier itself, Nendaz, Veysonnaz, La Tzoumaz and Thyon. Verbier is recognized as one of the premier 'off-piste' centres in the world. Consequently, many top skiers have chosen to settle permanently in the resort. The village lies on a south-orientated terrace facing the large glaciated massif of Grand Combin which includes the Grand Combin mountain (4,314 m) one of the highest peaks in the Alps and several other high peaks, including three more above 4,000 m. As with the section to Orsières, the line is standard gauge and its vehicles are powered by a 15kV AC supply. For more information about the train service to Le Châble and to Orsières, visit the website www.tmrsa.ch

## CH5 – Aigle to Leysin (AL)

More railways were established in the Chablais region in the cantons of Vaud and Valais following the opening of the Lausanne-Simplon railway in 1857. The town of Aigle was on this route and it quickly became a focal point for developing other railways to reach the communities in the nearby mountains. A metre gauge railway to the resort of Leysin route was one of the first to be built. In the late 19th century, the township of Leysin, with its excellent climate, became a health resort for the treatment of sufferers of tuberculosis. In those days, it took travellers between three and five hours to reach the resort by stagecoach. Discussions about constructing the railway began in 1880s with formal approval being granted by the end of 1898. No time was wasted in constructing the line leading to its official inauguration in November 1900. Over the following 15 years, Leysin saw significant development. In 1912, negotiations led to the opening of an extension of the line to the Grand Hotel de Leysin, the connection becoming operational in 1915. The line, overall, turned out to be very profitable not least of all for the revenues it earned from freight transport. However, with worldwide economic depression in the 1930s there came a downturn which led to the connection to Grand Hotel terminating in 1932; two years later, the hotel itself closed. After World War II, the fortunes of the line improved with Leysin increasingly becoming a major tourist destination with the development of ski lifts, an aerial tramway, a sports centre and other facilities. Today, Transports Publics du Chablais SA operates the railway. Services run from a recently re-furbished station alongside the main line station in Aigle. From Aigle (alt. 404 m) the train powered by a 1500V DC electricity supply, travels to Leysin (alt. 1,451 m) a total distance of 6.2 km. Given the height to be reached over a short distance (maximum gradient of 23 per cent) trains cannot climb without assistance. To overcome the problem on this metre gauge line an Abt designed rack/cogwheel system is utilized for just over 5 km of the journey. The journey to or from Leysin takes about 28 minutes. For more information, see the operator's website www.tpc.ch

St Bernard Express *en route* to Le Châble on 30th August, 2008.

*Caroline Jones*

Train travelling from Aigle to Leysin passing through the Vaud vineyards on 16th October, 2006.

*Author*

Various AOMC units parked at the railway's depot at Monthey on 16th October, 2006. *Author*

## CH6 – Aigle-Ollon-Monthey-Champéry (AOMC)

In 1897, the authorities approved the building of a railway line between Aigle and the villages of Ollon (alt. 468 m) and Villars (alt. 1,253 m). However, there was considerable disagreement about the route to be adopted. Eventually, in 1900, a concession was granted to build and operate a metre gauge railway from Aigle to Monthey (alt. 420 m) via Ollon. Villars was obliged to wait for its railway (*see entry CH 8*). Unfortunately, progress on constructing the line was slow compared to neighbouring railways, so it was not until April 1907 that the first trains began to operate on the line. The line was further extended from Monthey to the township of Champéry in early 1908. At the time, there was always the thought that the route would have a branch line from the village of Illiez to Morgins. However, because of doom and gloom forecasts of poor profitability and a looming war (World War I as it turned out to be) this section was not built. The final section of the route followed, more than 80 years later, when a 1 km track was opened from Champéry town to the Champéry-Planachaux lift. The benefit of this was to provide another link from the valley floor to the mountains. The route from Aigle to Champéry (alt. 1,049 m) following for much of the way the La Vièze river, climbs 645 m over a distance of 23.1 km. Over 3.6 km of this route, the gradient is as great as 13 per cent per cent, necessitating the aid of a rack/cogwheel system, this time one designed by Emil Strub. The railway is electrically powered (850V DC), has one tunnel (Troistorrents - length 193 m), six stations and 20 halts. Journey time is 62 minutes. Much of the route is through extensive vineyards. Transports Publics du Chablais SA is the operator of this railway (www.tpc.ch)

## CH7 – Aigle to Diablerets (ASD)

The last railway to be built from the Aigle terminus was the one to Les Diablerets (alt. 1,157 m) via Le Sépey (alt. 978 m). It was in 1905 that the Federal authorities granted the necessary approvals but ground was not broken and construction begun until 1911. There were serious civil engineering challenges in constructing this line including building the Vanel viaduct. This structure first required an aerial tramway to transport men and building materials and scaffolding across the Ormonts valley. This same scaffolding was later used to build the Les Planches viaduct further up the same line. The railway from Vers l'Eglise to Les Diablerets was opened in July 1914. The railway suffered a major setback in 1940 when its depot was destroyed by fire. As a result three electric-powered railcars and four passenger carriages were lost. There was serious talk of abandoning the railway at that time. Fortunately, positive decisions were made to recover as much as they could from the fire and lease rolling stock from other railway companies to keep services operating. Ideas were mooted in Bern, in 1985, for the Federal authorities to cease funding for all privately run railways; the ASD was likely to be a casualty. Fortunately, there was a re-think and subsequently a concession was granted until the year 2035. Attempts were made in 1996 by the Vaud canton and local communities to get the Federal Government to revoke this concession due to spiralling costs; again good fortune prevailed when the authorities in Bern recognised the importance of this railway and granted it status as a public transport carrier with guaranteed funding. The route of this railway is 22.3 km long but has gradients no greater than six per cent, and does not, therefore, need rack/cogwheel assistance. The metre gauge railway is electrically powered (1500V DC) and the journey takes 48 minutes each way. Transports Publics du Chablais SA is again the operator of this railway. See www.tpc.ch

ASD's railcar No. 402 heads for Aigle on 16th October, 2006.     *Author*

## CH8 – Bex to Col de Bretaye (BVB)

The Aigle-Leysin railway was not the first to operate in this area. In January 1898, a concession had been granted to the Bex authorities to build its line in three stages. The construction of the first part proceeded at breakneck speed as can be judged by the opening of the Bex (alt. 411 m) to Bevieux (alt. 483 m) section in September of that same year. The year 1900 saw the opening of the Bevieux to Gryon (alt. 1,131 m) section and a year later the final connection between Gryon and Villars (alt. 1,253 m). However, that was not the end of construction on the line. In 1905, the Federal authorities agreed to an extension to Chesières. Again, construction advanced quickly and the first train from Bex to Chesières ran in August 1906. A final section to the Col de Bretaye (alt. 1,813 m) opened in December 1913. The line from Bex to Col de Bretaye travels a distance of 17 km. There is one tunnel at Fontannaz-Seulaz (1,182 m), three stations and 10 halts. The line is electrically powered (700V DC) and because of the gradients up 20 per cent employs the Abt-designed rack/cogwheel system for 7.3 km of the route. The journey time from Bex to Villars is 40 minutes and from Villars to Col de Bretaye, a further 18 minutes. Transports Publics du Chablais SA is the operator. For more information, see www.tpc.ch

## CH9 – Chemin de Fer Legère de Rivière

Chemin de fer Legère de Riviere was formerly known as Chemins de Fer Électriques Veveysans (CEV). The CEV was formed in 1902 by the amalgamation of two railway companies, one providing services from Vevey to Blonay and the other from Blonay to Les Pléiades. In 1990, CEV became part of the Montreux Oberland Bernois railway (MOB) and is now part of the GoldenPass group of railway companies. This railway travels a route from Vevey, 18 km east of Lausanne, on the shores of Lake

Villars Palace Hotel with a BVB service heading for the nearby terminal on 16th October, 2006.

*Author*

A Vevey to Blonay service approaches the terminus on 17th October, 2006.

*Author*

Geneva, up to the large village of Blonay, a distance of 10 km. The railway then continues beyond the village for a further 4.8 km to Les Pléiades (alt. 1,348 m). Trains on the metre gauge line are electrically powered (900V DC) and because of the 20 per cent gradients beyond Chamby, the rack/cogwheel system designed by Emil Strub is employed. It takes 14 minutes to reach the village of Blonay (alt. 622 m) which, with a population of just over 5,000, is a tasteful dormitory suburb for Vevey and Montreux. There is a château at Blonay from which there are superb views of the lake and Mont Blanc Massif beyond. Continuing up the hill to the summit takes a further 20 minutes and a slightly longer 24 minutes coming down. An attractively-liveried powered railcar named *Astro Pléiades* is used for this part of the journey. From May to October each year, at the summit of Les Pléiades, offers an interesting exposition - *Astro Pléiades* - comprising four open-air exhibits pursuing various astronomical themes. The popular lakeside resort of Vevey is where Charlie Chaplin spent the last 25 years of his life. For more information about the rail services, visit www.mob.ch

## CH10 – Montreux Glion Rochers-de-Naye (MGN)

If the visitor is interested in marmots then this railway can help! It is understood that there are 14 species of marmot in the world, of which seven are kept in a natural environment in three separate parks at Rochers-de-Naye. Platform 8 at Montreux's main railway station is the departure point for regular trains throughout the year to climb 1,575 m in altitude to the terminus. The 7.6 km journey takes 55 minutes to complete. The line was built by two separate companies. In 1892, the Chemin de fer Glion-Rochers-de-Naye began services linking Glion, on the outskirts of Montreux, with Rochers-de-Naye (alt. 1,970 m) at the summit. Seventeen years later, the second company, opened the Chemin de fer Montreux-Glion route, making the connection from the main station to Glion which brought the added advantage of a connection with the Glion-Territet funicular. In 1987, the two companies merged to form the Chemin de fer de Montreux–Glion–Rochers-de-Naye which in 2001 was merged into Transports Montreux-Vevey-Riviera (MVR) and now part of the GoldenPass group of railway companies. Almost as soon as trains leave the environs of Montreux station, they begin to climb, and quite steeply at that. The first station to be reached is Glion, where the railway's depot is located. The train then continues up to the village of Caux and on to Parcot (alt. 1,430 m). Already the train has ascended 1,035 m in a travelling distance of 4.3 km. Over the next 3.3 km a further 540 m is added in height. To achieve such a steep climb, with gradients as great as 22 per cent, the Abt-designed rack/cogwheel system has to be employed on this narrow gauge (800 mm) line. The power to drive the trains is by an electricity supply of 850V DC picked up from overhead wires. For railway enthusiasts, Montreux is unusual in that it has three different gauges operating from the one station, a distinction it shares with Jenbach in Austria (*see entry A22*). Montreux is also famous for its music festivals and at one time its film festivals. On the promenade there is a superb life-size bronze of Freddie Mercury. For more information about this railway and the services it operates visit the website www.goldenpass.ch/default.asp?OrgID=7

Passing the Hotel des Alpes halt is MGN's No. 302 on 18th October, 2006. *Author*

Steam locomotive No. 105 at the Blonay-Chamby railway depot/museum on 22nd October, 2006.

*Author*

## CH11 – Chemin de Fer-Musée Blonay-Chamby

Standing above Montreux is the village of Blonay, from where one can enjoy excellent views of Lake Geneva. Close to Montreux in the direction of Villeneuve, is the picturesque Château de Chillon. The Château, built in the 11th century for the Dukes of Savoy, was immortalized in 1816 by Lord Byron in his poem *The Prisoner of Chillon*. The panoramic views are not the only attraction up here in Blonay. The route of this heritage railway is just over 3 km, running from near the Château of Blonay to the hamlet of Chamby. A museum belonging to this railway is said to have the largest collection of historic railway locomotives and carriages in Switzerland. The museum is located at Chamby, but it is not easy to find or access by road. The much preferred route is to travel to Blonay by road, or by rail from Vevey (*see entry CH9*) and take one of the railway's steam-hauled or electric-powered (900V DC) trains to Chamby. The trains, and for that matter, the museum, are active at weekends from May to October with extra services on Thursdays and Fridays in July and August. There are also 'specials' at various times of the year, Easter, for example. The journey on the metre gauge line takes 15 minutes and the cost of the ride includes entry to the museum. There is also a café and a souvenir shop. Overall, a visit to this heritage railway makes for an enjoyable half-day out. For more information, visit the railway's website at www.blonay-chamby.ch

## CH12 – St Gingolph to Martigny

Swiss Federal Railways (SBB) operates the regular services between St Gingolph and Martigny on the main line. St Gingolph is a small town situated on the southern shores of Lake Geneva. Almost one kilometre across the lake Vevey and Montreux can be seen. The town sits on the Swiss-Franco border and is believed to derive its name from the 8th century Saint Gangulphus who pursued a life locally as a hermit. The town played an important role during World War II when France's department Haute Savoie was occupied first by the Italian Army and later by the German forces. Given that St Gingolph was a border town, there were strong connections, often by marriage and work, between occupied France and neutral Switzerland. Much to the consternation of the occupying forces, this made it possible for a very active Resistance Movement to smuggle goods, arms and refugees (including many French Jews) across the border into Switzerland. St Gingolph is the terminus of the Swiss end of the line. On the French side the railway used to run from Evian-les-Bains (*see entry F16*) to St Gingolph. This railway line traces its history back to 1857 when it was part of the Chemin de fer d'Italie connecting France with Switzerland and Italy. The line carried passenger and goods traffic until 1938 and thereafter goods traffic only. Steam locomotives were operated on the line until 1954 when they were replaced by electric-powered traction. Services were finally withdrawn in May 1988. The trackbed still exists and there is a possibility of a re-opening of the line, perhaps in 2012, but that is far from certain in the prevailing economic climate. Asking a French railwayman (*cheminot*) about this possibility, all the author got was a gallic shrug! The line from St Gingolph is electrified and travels through Bouveret, Vouvry and Monthey over a distance of 26.8 km to join the main line at St Maurice just north of Martigny. At Bouveret is located the Swiss Vapeur Park (www.swissvapeur.ch) which is said to be Europe's most attractive miniature railway. It features an intricate passenger-carrying miniature railway that takes the visitors past many of Switzerland's famous beauty spots, albeit at 1/9th of their real size! The route is set in 17,000 square metres of exquisite parkland.

SBB service awaiting departure from St Gingolph station on 30th August, 2008.

*Author*

### CH13 – Golden Pass and Montreux-Oberland Bahn (MOB)

Montreux-Oberland Bahn (MOB) is one of the oldest electric-powered railway lines in Switzerland. The line opened progressively for rail services from Montreux to Zweisimmen between 1901 and 1905. In 1912, the Zweisimmen-Lenk line was developed. From the outset, the Montreux-Oberland Bahn took its railway seriously introducing dining and saloon coaches, for example. As consequence of the Depression in the early 1930s, the by-then Golden Mountain Pullman Express service was hit hard and drastic measures had to be taken to survive, including selling off some of the rolling stock. Today, the successor to that early luxury train is the Crystal Panoramic Express. Leaving Montreux station (alt. 395 m) on its metre-wide track and powered by a 900V DC electricity supply, the train, one of the three each day in each direction, winds its way up through the vineyards above Lake Geneva. It continues to climb through Chamby to Les Avants, the village where Nöel Coward lived for 14 years. After running through the tunnel under the Col de Jaman (1,512 m) and emerging into the remote Hongrin valley, it reaches the Saane river valley which it then follows upstream. Leaving the French-speaking canton of Vaud it then enters the German-speaking canton of Bern. After reaching Gstaad it climbs the Saanenmöser Pass, which at 1,279 m, is the highest point on the line; thereafter, it descends to the town of Zweisimmen (alt. 941 m). The total distance travelled has been 75 km. The maximum gradient is 7.3 per cent which is climbed without rack/cogwheel assistance. Montreux-Oberland Bahn with its GoldenPass services was the world's first railway to deploy panoramic trains. These allow some passengers, the so-called VIPs, to sit at the front of the train under the driver's compartment and share the driver's view of the route ahead. For more see: www.goldenpass.ch

### CH14 – Bernese Oberland Bahn (BOB)

The Bernese Oberland Bahn, with its distinctive yellow and blue liveried trains, operates services from Interlaken (alt. 564 m) to Grindelwald (alt. 1,034 m) and Lauterbrunnen (alt. 797 m). A combined train leaves Interlaken Ost and travels to Zweilutschinen (alt. 652 m) where the depot headquarters and the main workshops are located. Here, it divides with one part of the train going up to Grindelwald and the other to Lauterbrunnen. All the route is electrified (1500V DC) and the gauge of the track is metre-wide. Gradients of up to 12 per cent are encountered on the route necessitating rack/cogwheel assistance based on the design by Niklaus Riggenbach. The railway began operations in 1890 and was electrified in 1914. In 1999, a 2.5 km section of double track was laid between Zweilutschinen and Wilderswil to reduce delays by allowing trains to pass. Today, the railway plays a vital part in the Interlaken's railway network by facilitating fast, reliable transport to key tourist locations. Grindelwald (population 3,760) is the usual starting point for ascents of the Eiger (3,970 m) and the Wetterhorn (3,692 m). From Lauterbrunnen (population 2,663) known for its numerous local waterfalls, it is possible to take the Wengernalpbahn (*see entry CH17*) which gives access to Kleine Scheidegg from where the Jungfraubahn departs (*see entry CH18*). More information about the services this railway operates can be obtained from the parent website www.jungfraubahn.ch

### CH15 – Gornergratbahn

The Gornergratbahn runs between Zermatt and the Gornergrat mountain station. However, because road traffic is not allowed to travel into Zermatt it is necessary for those travelling by car to transfer to a shuttle train from the last point to which one can drive, Täsch. The line from Zermatt to Gornergrat measures 9.34 km with

GoldenPass train with panoramic coach at the rear on 17th October, 2006 heads down to Montreux with no 'VIPs' taking advantage of seeing where they have just been!

*Author*

A BOB service heads for Interlaken from Lauterbrunnen on 9th October, 2006.

*Author*

A Gornergrat service descends 'on the rack' from Riffelberg station on 12th October, 2006.

*Author*

intermediate stations at Riffelalp, Riffelberg and Rotenboden. It is possible to alight at any station and walk down all or part of the way, or for that matter, hike up! The full journey by train takes 40 minutes. As is common to many Swiss railways in the Alps steep climbs are inevitably encountered. The maximum gradient of 20 per cent on the Gornergrat is no exception. To overcome the difficulty where normal adhesion would not be appropriate, a rack/cogwheel system, designed by Roman Abt, is used on this double track metre gauge line. The electric power supply is three phase 725V 50Hz. On reaching Gornergrat's top station, there is no shortage of impressive mountains to see. For example, the Gornergrat itself standing at 3,130 m is an ideal platform to appreciate the Dom (4,545 m), Weißhorn (4,505 m), Dent Blanche (4,356 m), Lyskamm (4,527 m) and the Monte Rosa, which at an altitude of 4,634 m, is the second highest mountain in the Alps. From the Gornergrat, on a clear day, it is possible to see as many as twenty 4000+ metre high peaks! However, the crowning glory must go to the iconic Matterhorn (4,478 m). Whilst it is not the highest peak in the Alps, its 1,200 m north face presents one of the greatest climbing challenges. It is also one of the deadliest with a tragic record of claiming the lives of over 500 alpinists between 1865 and 1995 and more since. It is perhaps a little surprising to learn that in the early 1890s there was much opposition to the building of this railway. This came mainly from local politicians who thought the local economy and, in particular, the employment of mountain guides and porters would be adversely affected. Notwithstanding, the railway was eventually built and services began operating in 1898. The Gornergrat claims the record of being the first electric-powered mountain railway to be constructed in Switzerland. For more information about this railway, see www.gornergrat.ch

## CH16 – Schynige-Platte Bahn

Standing at 584 m above sea level is the large village of Wilderswil, 3 km south of Interlaken. It can be accessed by road and by the Bernese Oberland Bahn (*see entry CH14*). From Wilderswil a railway takes the traveller to the Schynige Platte (alt. 1,987 m) considered by many to be one of the best vantage points in the whole region, although the author has to say that the Gornergrat takes some beating. As the train ascends, the landscape is varied, first with dense forests and then fertile alpine pastures. Finally, the traveller is rewarded with a ringside seat of the Bernese Oberland with the Eiger (3,970 m), the Mönch (4,099 m) and the Jungfrau (4,158 m) mountains standing there in all their majesty. Schynige Platte is a high plateau from which one also has superb views of the two lakes at Interlaken, the Thunersee and the Brienzersee. As with the Gornergrat, this is not an experience to be missed, summer or winter. A special garden is located near the summit where various alpine plants can be found. Near to the railway station is a hotel and mountain restaurant. Schynige Platte is also the starting point for the popular hiking trials to the Faulhorn (2,681 m) and the First (2,166 m). The Schynige-Platte Bahn was inaugurated in June 1893. Trains were at first hauled by steam-powered locomotives, but not for long, as the narrow gauge line (800 mm) was electrified (1500V DC) in 1914. Many of the carriages and locomotives used today originally started out their careers with the Wengernalpbahn (*see entry CH17*). Some of this rolling stock is returned to that railway in the winter months to help meet the heavy increases in seasonal tourist traffic. The distance that railway travels is not long, 7.2 km, but it does take an enjoyable 45 minutes to reach the final destination. The reason for this is that the gradients are as much as 25 per cent requiring assistance from the Riggenbach-Pauli rack/cogwheel system. More information for this railway and others can be found on the main Jungfraubahnen site at www.jungfraubahn.ch

Riggenbach's rack can be seen here clearly as a Schynige-Platte Bahn service descends to Wilderswil on 11th October, 2006. *Author*

The Eiger looks down on a Wengernalpbahn train as it drops down to Lauterbrunnen from Kleine Scheidegg, 9th October, 2006. *Caroline Jones*

## CH17 – Wengernalpbahn

Wengernalpbahn is the longest continuous cogwheel railway in the world. The railway runs between Lauterbrunnen and Kleine Scheidegg and between Kleine Scheidegg and Grindelwald. The overall length of the line is 19.09 km. However, trains do not travel that distance directly from Lauterbrunnen to Grindelwald or vice versa. The reason for this is one of safety. The powered railcars are always located at the lower end of the train composition pushing up the carriages rather than pulling them. This means that trains do not pass through Kleine Scheidegg and down the other side to Lauterbrunnen as that would put the motive power, and therefore braking influence, at the wrong end of the train. The same applies to the trains from Lauterbrunnen to Kleine Scheidegg. In 1948, a triangular section of track was built into the side of the mountain at Kleine Scheidegg which makes it possible for the powered railcars to be re-positioned and used on the other side of the pass. The busiest section on the railway is the 3 km from Lauterbrunnen to Wengen. The normal population of this village is 1,300 but rises to over 5,000 in summer and 10,000 in winter. Wengen stands at an altitude of 1,274 m and is a traffic-free zone meaning that the railway plays the key role in the transportation of people and goods to and from the village. Between Wengen and Kleine Scheidegg is the village of Wengeralp where at times Mendelssohn, Wagner and Tchaikovsky all spent holidays. Lord Byron also stayed in the village and where, it is said, he found the inspiration to write his poem *Manfred*. Construction of the track began in 1891 and the route officially opened in June 1893. Using steam-powered locomotives for a number of years, it was electrified (1500V DC) between 1909 and 1910. The track for this railway is narrow gauge (800 mm) and to negotiate the maximum gradient of 25 per cent the railway operates on the Riggenbach-Pauli rack/cogwheel system, which, it is understood, is in the process of being converted to the double lamella system (Abt). Kleine Scheidegg is the departure station for the Jungfraujoch (*see next entry*). The website for this line is off the main Jungfraubahnen site www.jungfraubahn.ch

## CH18 – Jungfraubahn

Construction of the Jungfraubahn first began in 1898 and subsequently opened in stages. However, because of financial difficulties encountered during the building of a long tunnel, it took the constructors seven years to build the final section from Eismeer to Jungfraujoch. Consequently, it was not until 1912 that the village of Jungfraujoch was eventually reached and rail services could begin to operate. Unlike the Wengernalpbahn, which was built using 800 mm gauge, the designers of this railway decided to chose metre gauge. This was installed with the then new rack/cogwheel system designed by Emil Strub to negotiate the 25 per cent gradients. Initially, the Jungfraubahn operated on a three-phase electricity supply with a line voltage of 500V 40Hz but this was later changed to what is today's supply, 1125V 50Hz. The route of the railway is from Kleine Scheidegg, accessed via the Wengernalpbahn, to the Jungfraujoch, a total distance of 11.8 km of which 9.3 km is used for the journey. There are six stations/halts and two tunnels on the route. The journey takes 52 minutes. The mountain terminus at the Jungfraujoch houses two underground station halls and at an altitude of 3,454 m makes it Europe's highest railway station. The tunnel, that earlier had slowed construction work, is 7 km long and burrows through the Eiger and the Mönch mountains. In the tunnel there are two intermediate stations blasted out of the rock, one at Eigerwand (alt. 2,864 m) and the other at Eismeer (alt. 3,158 m). Both stations have panoramic windows affording awe-inspiring views of the Alps. They are not to be missed. A few of the old locomotive-hauled 'rowan-trains' are still kept in reserve and are occasionally used to meet heavy demand. Incidentally, one of these rowan-trains from the early days of the Jungfraubahn's operations, and similar to those that were used on the Gornergratbahn, is preserved on display in the Transport Museum at Luzern. Today, regular traffic is handled by 14 railcars with matching trailers. For more information, see www.jungfraubahn.ch

An ascent begins to the Jungfraujoch station on 11th October, 2006. *Author*

The freight depot at Murren on 11th October, 2006. *Author*

## CH19 – Bergbahn Lauterbrunnen-Murren

Whilst this route is one of the Jungfraubahn group of railways, there is no direct connection with any other of the services operated. Standing at an altitude of 690 m above Lauterbrunnen is the village of Grütschalp (alt. 1,487 m) from where the trains run on metre gauge track to Murren (alt. 1,639) a distance of 4.3 km. It is single track with a passing point mid-way. The journey takes 14 minutes. The trackbed is reasonably level except for a section near Winteregg where the gradient is five per cent, but this is managed without rack/cogwheel assistance. Rolling stock comprises three 4-axle electrically-powered railcars operating on a power supply of 550V DC. They are maintained at workshops at Grütschalp. Access to the railway for visitors is by cable car (capacity 100 persons) from Lauterbrunnen to Grütschalp. The distance covered is 1.4 km in just four minutes. This cable car was opened in 2006 to replace the previous funicular which had become dangerously unsafe due to water and geological problems. The only other access to Murren, a car-free town like Zermatt, is also by cable car from Stechelberg further up the valley. The history of the railway goes back over 100 years. A concession to build the railway was granted in 1887 and construction began two years later. The railway opened in 1891. It had been intended that it would operate from the June of that year but a derailment caused a delay until the August. The views from this railway are stunning. Behind the railway (to the east) is the Bietenhorn (2,757 m), the Schilltorn also as known as Piz Gloria (2,970 m), the Drättehorn (2,794 m) and the Sulegg (2,413 m) mountains. Facing the railway, across the valley, is the Kleine Scheidegg plateau and the mountains of Männlichen (2,343 m), Eiger (3,970 m), Mönch (4,099 m) and Jungfrau (4,158 m). For more information about this railway, consult the parent website: www.jungfraubahn.ch

## CH20 – Brünig Bahn

Up until 2006, the Brünig Bahn, name coming from the Brünig Pass (alt. 1,008 m) it crosses, was, at one time, the only narrow metre gauge line operated by the Swiss Federal Railways (SBB). Operating in conjunction with the Montreux-Oberland Bernois Railway (MOB) (see entry CH13) the railway serves a route known as the 'Golden Pass of Switzerland'. The railway is now operated by the private concession die Zentralbahn. The railway running between Luzern and Interlaken Ost is over a distance of 73 km with the journey taking between 90 and 150 minutes depending upon the service taken. The line runs from Luzern passing Alpnachstad to Giswil where it climbs the 10 per cent gradient using the rack/cogwheel system designed by Niklaus Riggenbach. From Giswil the line climbs to the station at Brünig-Hasliberg (1,002 m) then drops down a 12.1 per cent gradient to the floor of the valley at Meiringen, the mid-point on the route. From Meiringen, the line runs across the valley and along the shores of Lake Brienz to Interlaken Ost. Trains are electrically powered by an overhead supply of 15kV AC. The railway was first built in 1888, when it then linked Brienz with Alpnachstad. Later, in 1889, it was extended to Luzern and finally, in 1913, the Brienz to Interlaken 'lake line' section was opened. From the outset and until 1941-42, steam traction operated on the line before the conversion to the AC electric power system. Steam-hauled trains return to line from time to time operated by Ballenberg Dampfbahn from Interlaken (see entry CH29). Whilst much of the route is enclosed in woodland there are ample opportunities to see the surrounding, often snow-capped, mountains of Giswilerstock (2,011 m), Wilerhorn (2,004 m), Chingstuel (2,118 m) and the Tschingel (2,322 m).

Meiringen station on 3rd February, 2007 with Ballenberg Dampfbahn's rack/cogwheel locomotive No. 1067 re-fuelling before making an ascent of the Brünig Bahn.

*Author*

## CH21 – Brienz-Rothorn Bahn

This line is one of Switzerland's earliest rack/cogwheel-assisted railways having been first opened in 1892. With the opening in 1888 of the nearby Brünig Bahn (*see previous entry*) the idea of a constructing a mountain railway to the summit of the Brienzer Rothorn (alt. 2,350 m) became a reality. Work began in 1890 and was completed two years later. The two designers, engineer Lindner and building contractor Bertschinger, were helped by the railway engineer Roman Abt, who installed on the line his then newly-developed double lamella rack/cogwheel system. After its opening, the railway quickly achieved success carrying over 11,000 passengers in its first season. However, dark clouds were on the horizon as the company encountered financial difficulties. Competition with the Schynige-Platte Bahn (*see entry CH16*) which had opened in 1893 and the Jungfraubahn a little later, took the much-needed custom away. The financial problems were further compounded with the outbreak of World War I in 1914. Consequently, a decision was taken to close the line at the beginning of August 1914. It remained closed for 16 years. In 1931, ironically at a high point in the Depression, a new company was formed to resurrect the railway. It was successful. During the 1940s and 1950s, many other railways embarked upon programmes of electrification. However, Brienz-Rothorn Bahn decided on a radical alternative, i.e. to retain its steam-hauled trains. For this, it was helped by the Furka Cogwheel Steam Railway (*see entry CH28*) the only railway company at that time still running regular steam operations in Switzerland. However, because of the age and general condition of the original steam locomotives, it was necessary for Brienz-Rothorn Bahn to supplement the fleet by purchasing four diesel-fuelled locomotives in order to maintain services. Regular steam, however, did eventually return in 1992, when the Swiss locomotive manufacturer, SLM at Winterthur, built three brand new steam locomotives for the railway. The Brienz-Rothorn Bahn was not the only railway

company to see the commercial benefits of steam. Newly-constructed locomotives were also supplied to the Montreux-Glion-Rochers-de-Naye railway (*see entry CH10*) and to two railways in Austria - the Schneebergbahn (*see entry A8*) and the Schafbergbahn (*see entry A32*). The steam locomotives are oil-fired which allows for one-man operation bringing obvious economies to the company's tourist operations. For more information, see www.brienz-rothorn-bahn.ch

## CH22 – Meiringen-Innertkirchen Bahn (MIB)

The village of Meiringen (population 4,740) is located near Reichenbachfälle - the waterfalls at which Arthur Conan Doyle set the story of 'the struggle to the death' between his detective Sherlock Holmes and the villainous Professor Moriarty. To commemorate this fictional event, there is a Sherlock Holmes Museum in the basement of the deconsecrated English church in Meiringen. It is open from May to September every afternoon except on Mondays. A funicular built in 1899 named the Reichenbachfällbahn takes interested visitors to the 'scene of the murder'. Meiringen's other claim to fame is the meringue. There is a delightful *patisserie* and *café du thé* on the main street of the town where one can buy and consume this local delicacy. The private metre gauge railway (electrified at 1200V DC) takes 11 minutes to travel from Meiringen to the village of Innertkirchen (population 960) a distance of 5 km. There are two tunnels on the route one of which is the 1,502 m-long Kirchentunnel which bypasses the Aare gorge. The railway owes its origins to the development of local hydropower plants. At the beginning of the 20th century, plans were implemented to harness water energy to generate electric power in the nearby Oberhasli and Grimsel passes. To facilitate this objective, a narrow gauge railway was planned from Meiringen to Guttannen via Innertkirchen. In 1926, the railway between Meiringen and Innertkirchen was completed allowing for transportation of building materials and construction workers. However, for economic reasons the final section from Innertkirchen to Guttannen was never built. From the beginning, there

A cheerful lady driver greets the author/photographer with a wave as the Brienz-Rothorn train begins its journey to the summit from Brienz station on 8th October, 2006.

*Author*

An early afternoon service from Meiringen heads for Innertkirchen on 3rd February, 2006.    *Author*

The Vitznau terminus of the Rigi Bahnen on 8th October, 2006.

*Author*

was no passenger traffic other than for construction workers and their families as no official approval having been given. However, this changed in 1946 when the Swiss Federal Government granted formal permission and so the Meiringen-Innertkirchen Bahn was born. This railway's departure point in the town of Meiringen is a short distance from the main die Zentralbahn station. But there is no direct connection between the two railways owing to their differing electrical power systems. For more, visit www.grimselwelt.ch/bahnen/meiringen-innertkirchen-bahn

### CH23 – Rigi Bahnen

The ascent of the Rigi (alt. 1,798 m) near Luzern is achieved by using one of two railways jointly operated by the Rigi Bahnen Company. The first one, opened in 1871, is the route from Vitznau on the shores of Vierwaldestätter See (also known as Lake Luzern or Lucerne) to the top station at Rigi Kulm (alt. 1,752 m). This is the oldest rack/cogwheel railway in the world. The standard gauge line is electrified (1500V DC) and to climb the 25 per cent gradient trains employ the Riggenbach system. The same system is used to climb the maximum gradient of 20 per cent on the other side of the Rigi from Arth-Goldau close to the Zuger See. This second route was opened in 1875. At 6.9 km, the route from Vitznau is shorter of the two by 1.7 km. Whilst electrically-powered railcars are the norm, there are still some steam-driven services operated during July and September. A memorial dedicated to Riggenbach and his invention can be seen at Vitznau station. At the summit, there is a café and shop, an ideal starting point for the many walks on the Rigi. The mountain is known as the 'Queen of the Mountains' and from the summit station and on the walks, the views are superb all seasons and in all directions. The trains have no difficulty in taking wheelchairs and prams. There is plenty of parking at Vitznau, Goldau and Weggis. Half-hourly services operate daily throughout the year. For more information, see the website: www.rigi.ch

### CH24 – Pilatus Bahn

With so many routes operating rack/cogwheel systems in Switzerland it should not come as any surprise to learn that the country happens to have the steepest railway in the world. The honour belongs to the Pilatus Bahn near Luzern. The metre gauge railway runs from Alpnachstad (alt. 436 m) on the shores of the Alpnachersee to Pilatus Kulm (alt. 2,073 m) a distance of 4.6 km. The trains take 30 minutes to make the ascent. The rack/cogwheel system used to achieve this challenging climb was one designed by Eduard Locher. It operates with two horizontally revolving cogwheels engaging the rack rail. It is the only one of this type in use in Switzerland. The maximum gradient Locher's system overcomes is an amazing 48 per cent. The railway was opened in 1889 and operated steam traction until 1937, the journey time then being 70 minutes. The delay, compared with today's much quicker timings, was caused by the need to stop and take water at the passing station at Aemsigen. In May 1937, following the introduction of electrification to the line, the journey time was reduced to 30 minutes. As a matter of interest, one of those early steam-driven railcars is on static display in the Swiss Transport Museum not very far away in the city of Luzern. The railway operates all the year round except for the first two weeks in November when it is closed for a programme of annual maintenance. From May to October each year, the railway offers the 'Golden Round Trip' which comprises a 1st or 2nd class boat trip from Luzern to Alpnachstad, then up to Pilatus Kulm, down to Kriens by gondola cableway and finally back to Luzern. In good weather, the views of the Alps and Central Switzerland's lakeland landscape are not to be missed. More information can be obtained from www.pilatus.ch

On 8th October, 2006 even the access steps seem steep on the world's steepest railway! *Author*

## CH25 – Luzern-Stans-Engelberg

The independent railway company, die Zentralbahn, operates a number of rail services in central Switzerland including the Brünig Bahn (*see entry CH20*). This route, from the city of Luzern (population 57,890) to the resort of Engelberg (population 4,001) is particularly interesting and popular. From Luzern, the metre gauge line travels to Hergiswil before briefly going underground (under the Vierwaldstätter See) to Stans (population 7,579). Incidentally, it is from Stans that the Stanserhorn funicular operates. The line continues to the village of Obermatt (alt. 675 m) where the Riggenbach rack/cogwheel system is engaged taking trains up the 24.6 per cent gradient to Ghärst. From there, trains continue unaided to Engelberg. The trains are powered by a 15kV AC electricity supply delivered by overhead catenaries. The total distance is 24.8 km and takes 53 minutes. The railway started life life in 1898 as the Stansstad-Engelberg railway (StEB). The line was electrified with three phase current, which was used by both the 'valley' railcars on the plain and the 'mountain' locos. On the plain, traffic was handled by electric-powered railcars but for the connection with Engelberg these railcars had to be pushed up the incline by small HGe 2/2 electric locomotives. Owing to the failure or inability to replace the ageing rolling stock coupled with a loss of traffic, the StEB went into bankruptcy in 1964. That same year, a new company was formed Luzern-Stans-Engelberg (LSE) and a decision was made to renew track and rolling stock. A tunnel was also built which allowed for a connection from Stans to Hergiswil. This made it possible to connect Stans directly with Luzern by sharing the track with the then SBB-operated Brünig line. This co-operative arrangement continued until the private railway operator, die Zentralbahn, took over the responsibility in January 2005. A 4 km tunnel is currently being constructed on the route to Engelberg in order to make for easier working by reducing the maximum gradient to be climbed. However, the completion of the project is delayed owing to geological/water difficulties. For more information, see www.zentralbahn.ch

An LSE electric railcar No. BDeh 4/4 5 standing at Engelberg station on 7th October, 2006.                                                                                     *Author*

MGB's electric locomotive No. Deh 4/4 94 *Fiesch* arrives at Göschenen station on 30th September, 2006.

*Author*

## CH26 – Matterhorn-Gotthard Bahn (MGB)

The Matterhorn-Gotthard Bahn was formed on 1st January, 2003 as a result of a merger of the former Brig-Visp-Zermatt-Bahn (BVZ) and Furka-Oberalp Bahn (FO). The history of these two railways goes back to the late 19th and early 20th centuries. From the 1860s, the mountains near Zermatt had increasingly gained noteriety with climbers and explorers. The Matterhorn became a huge attraction after Edward Whymper had made the first successful climb in 1865. To benefit from this new found tourism, in 1886, two Swiss banks collaborated and sought approval to build a railway to Zermatt from the town of Visp; the line was opened in July 1891. Thus, the Visp-Zermatt (VZ) railway was established but expansion further east by connecting with the Furkabahn Brig Furka Disentis (BFD) railway was not possible until Brig and Visp had been connected in 1930. This final connection made it possible later for the inauguration of the Glacier Express service (*see next entry*). By this time, the then re-named BVZ route had been electrified (11kV AC) throughout its 43.9 km length. This enabled the introduction of what became known as the almost legendary 'Krokodil' electric locomotives. The other company involved, the Furka Oberalp Bahn, began in May 1910 and by 1915 the Brig to Gletsch route was opened. However, further development of the line to Andermatt and Disentis was delayed by the problems encountered in building the Furka Scheiteltunnel and the onset of World War I. The problems did not ease and eventually led to a financial crisis in the company causing bankruptcy in 1923. Happily, in 1924, the project was rescued and by October of the following year, just before the onset of the winter snows, the first train travelled the entire route from Brig to Disentis. The traction at this time was steam-driven but it was not until the early 1940s that the line was electrified with the financial aid of the Swiss Federation and the muscle of the Swiss military. Electrification, however, did not overcome the suspension of the services in the winter. The weather conditions were regularly so severe on the Furka Pass route that the overhead power lines had to be dismantled every autumn and re-assembled the following spring! It was some 40 years before services became a year-round operation. This was in 1982, when the 15.5 km-long Furka base tunnel was opened. MGB now operates five principal routes, viz. Disentis to Brig; Andermatt to Göschenen; Brig to Zermatt via Visp; car transport between Realp and Oberwald through the Furka base tunnel; and the shuttle service between Täsch and Zermatt. MGB also operates, in conjunction with the Rhätische Bahn (*see entry CH30*), the Glacier Express. Overall, the MGB network amounts to 144 km. Gradients of up to 17.9 per cent are encountered which are addressed, where necessary, by the Abt-designed rack/cogwheel system. See the website www.mgb.ch

## CH27 – The Glacier Express

One of the most famous great railway journeys of the world is the Glacier Express. It travels from Zermatt in the canton of Valais to Chur, Davos or St Moritz in the Graubünden canton, a distance of 291 km. 'Express' it is not, as it takes almost eight hours to reach any one of its destinations but the scenery for the whole of the journey is legendary, so who is watching the clock? The first Glacier Express began in 1930, hauled from the outset by electric traction, the journey in those days taking up to 11 hours. Much of the route traces its origins back to 1890 when Jan Holsboer, a Dutchman, opened a line between Landquart and Davos. The company which ran this line later became the Rhätische Bahn (*see entry CH30*) and over the coming years the townships of Chur, Thusis and St Moritz were added to the network. St Moritz's fame is well understood but Chur and Thusis also have their claims. Chur was where Angelica Kauffmann was born. She emigrated to England in 1766 and later founded the Royal Academy. Thusis is one for art connoisseurs. Nearby is the Via Mala,

The Glacier Express crossing the Furkareuss II viaduct near Hospental on 30th September, 2006.

*Author*

a very narrow dramatic valley which has been recorded on canvas several times by Turner. Back to the railway, further expansion followed to include other towns and in 1922 the network was electrified. Other important players in the development of this line to the west were Brig-Visp-Zermatt Bahn (BVZ) and the Furka-Oberalp Bahn (FO), these later becoming part of the Matterhorn-Gotthard Bahn (*see previous entry*). Up until the early 1980s, the service only ran in the summer months because of the adverse winter conditions on the passes. That changed, as previously reported, when the Furka base tunnel was opened in 1982. The tunnel, together with the acquisition of improved locomotives developed in the 1980s and 1990s, has meant that the journey times have been reduced to what they are today. There is much to see and admire on the route; for example, there are 91 tunnels and 291 bridges including the famous Landwasser viaduct near Filisur. The tallest structure on the route, at a height of 85 m, is the Solis bridge crossing the River Albula. The railway is metre gauge and trains operate by normal adhesion aided only in three places by Abt's rack/cogwheel system. Those locations are the Matter valley between Stalden and Zermatt (maximum gradient of 12½ per cent), the Oberalp Pass (gradient 11 per cent) and in the Goms between Andermatt and Brig (gradient up to 9 per cent). The Glacier Express operates with 1st and 2nd class panoramic coaches built by the Swiss manufacturer Stadler as well as conventional coaches. The panoramic coaches are obviously superior not only for their better viewing opportunities but they are also air-conditioned. A commentary along the route is given in German, French, English, Italian, Chinese and Japanese languages. More information can be found at www.glacierexpress.ch

## CH28 – Dampfbahn Furka Bergstrecke

The rail and road route from Realp (alt. 1,538 m) near Andermatt over the Furka Pass (alt. 2,431 m) to Gletsch passes the magnificent glacier which is the source of the River Rhône and the primary feed for Lake Geneva, 155 km downstream. Sadly, it is receding, and at a rate which has been more rapid in recent decades. Local villages such as Gletsch depend on the Rhône Glacier to attract tourists. However, so great has the decline been that locals from the village now make strenuous efforts every summer to slow the melting process by covering the lower end with insulating blankets. So perhaps now is the time that the concerned traveller should take this steam-driven rail journey before too much more of the glacier is lost forever. The heavy winter snows on the Furka Pass make it impossible for any railway to guarantee operations other than from late June to early October each year. Consequently, on Fridays, Saturdays and Sundays during that period supplemented by daily services from mid-July to mid-August there is a fantastic opportunity to travel the line from Realp, close to the entrance to Furka base Tunnel, over the pass to Gletsch, a distance of 13 km. There are 11 bridges on the route, including the famous Steffenbach bridge constructed in 1925 (re-built 1988) and five tunnels one being the 1,858 m-long summit tunnel. The line's gauge is metre wide with steam locomotives relying on Roman Abt's rack/cogwheel system to climb the maximum gradient of 11 per cent. As already said, the original service on the route met its end in 1982. The plan, at that time, was to remove the old track but fortunately, some railway enthusiasts managed to save it. In 1983, Verein Furka-Bergstrecke (VFB) was founded aimed at restoring the route. A little later, the Furka Cogwheel Steam Railway organization was created with the objective of returning steam traction to the line. In 1992, came the re-opening of the first part of the line from Realp to Tiefenbach and in 1993, an extension to the Furka station. In 1996, the reconstruction of the Furka tunnel was completed making it possible to re-establish full services between Realp and Gletsch. It is hoped that the line will be eventually re-opened beyond Gletsch to Oberwald thus adding a further 6 km to this delightful railway. For more see the website www.dampfbahnen.ch

Dampfbahn Furka Bergstreke's steam locomotive No. 9 *Gletschhorn* has emerged from the Furka tunnel and is dropping down towards Gletsch on 30th September, 2006. Facing the train is the roadway descending from the highest point on the Furka Pass. Out of shot and behind the first 'hill' is the Rhône Glacier. *Author*

## CH29 – Ballenberg-Dampfbahn

From its workshop and offices at the far eastern end of Interlaken Ost station members of the Ballenberg-Dampfbahn meet to restore and operate steam locomotives. They own a number of locomotives and in particular regularly deploy two beautifully restored Swiss-built (SLM Winterthur) locomotives, viz. No. 1067 built in 1926 and No. 208 built in 1913. Both are coal-fired. It is possible by prior arrangement to view the excellent, well-equipped and spotlessly clean Ballenberg-Dampfbahn workshops. There, the steam locomotive C 5/6 (four cylinder compound) No. 2969 *Erstfeld* is in the course of meticulous restoration. The association, on certain Sundays during the summer months (July to September), operate excursions on the Brünig Bahn (*see entry CH20*). The trains, comprising a steam locomotive and vintage carriages, leave Interlaken Ost and travel east down the valley to Meiringen, arriving there about 90 minutes later. There is a break of about half an hour perhaps to enjoy a meringue with coffee from the nearby *patisserie* whilst the locomotive takes its own refreshment, water and coal. The train then leaves Meiringen heading for the Brünig Pass, it is not long before one hears the 'clunk' of the locomotive's cogwheel engaging with Riggenbach's rack rail. It takes about 20 minutes to reach the highest point at Brünig-Hasliberg station (alt. 1,002 m) where there is another half-hour break giving the opportunity to step off the train and admire the views. Back on the train, the traveller continues down to Giswil, the end of the journey. A pleasurable four hours have been spent since leaving Interlaken. Ninety minutes or so are allowed to tour the village, to take lunch at a restaurant or picnic, and perhaps visit the two nearby ruins of Rosenberg and Rudenz. Mid-afternoon the train makes its return by the outward route arriving at Interlaken about 1800 hours. A splendid day out, irrespective whether or not one is a railway enthusiast. Ballenberg-Dampfbahn offer their train services for special charters. UK's Railway Touring Company, for example, has taken advantage of this opportunity on a number of occasions. For more information, visit the website at www.dampfbahnen.ch

Ballenberg Dampfbahn's steam locomotive No. 1067 speeds alongside the River Aare towards Meiringen on 3rd February, 2007.

*Author*

The famous Landwasser viaduct near Filisur on 4th October, 2006.

*Author*

## CH30 – Rhätische Bahn (RhB)

Rhätische Bahn (en. Rhaetian Railway) operates an important 384 km-long rail network in Eastern Switzerland much of it being in Graubünden. More than a century ago, officials in the canton of Graubünden had a wish to construct a railway line through the Splügen valley into Italy calling upon the federal authorities to assist. After much debate the federal government decided to back the building of the Gotthard route even though it entailed the construction of a 15 km tunnel. Not to be put off, the Graubünden canton decided to build its own rail network with the objective of allowing easier access to its 150 valleys. So, in the late 18th and early 19th centuries a large narrow-gauge system was constructed with the first step being taken by the Dutchman, Jan Holsboer, who was the owner of a hotel in Davos. He thought that a railway would bring considerably greater numbers of tourists to the area than the horse-drawn carriages and mail coaches would ever be able to do. The Landquart-Davos Railway (LD) was founded, and in 1889, a line was opened as far as Klosters, reaching Davos a year later. The Davos-Filisur section was opened in 1909 followed by another line connecting Chur with St Moritz via Thusis, Filisur and Albula. One of the best-known structures, the Landwasser viaduct near Filisur, was built at this time. Various other lines were constructed and with the route from Scuol to Tarasp opened in 1913, the network was more or less complete. Today the network is all electrified operating on a supply of 11kV AC. In addition to operating its modern fleet of locomotives and railcars in their distinctive red livery, a number of historic vehicles, including steam traction, have been preserved and are used occasionally for excursions. Many of the services operated by the Rhätische Bahn go under various names, for example, the Engadin Star, Arosa Express, Albula Line, Aqualino Scuol, Vereina Line and Railrider. Then, of course, are the world famous Bernina and Glacier Expresses. In 2008, the Rhätische Bahn was added to the UNESCO list of World Heritage sites. For more information about this marvellous railway, visit the website www.rhb.ch

## CH31 – Bernina Express

The Bernina Pass route to Tirano, just over the border in Italy, opened in 1906. It was intended only to be a tourist railway and for that reason rail services were restricted to the summer. However, it was not that many years before the route became an all year round operation in order to meet the needs of the outlying Puschlav Valley (it. Val Poschiavo). For several decades the Bernina route represented the only viable connection in winter between the Puschlav and other parts of Switzerland. The Bernina line crosses the Alps attaining altitudes of more than 2,000 m as trains pass by the impressive Piz Bernina (alt. 4,049 m). Trains manage these climbs by adhesion only and without the aid of a rack/cogwheel system even though maximum gradients are quite steep in places, as much as 7.14 per cent. Another hazard, of course, is snow. This means that for much of the year considerable effort has to be made to keep the line open even under the most adverse and hostile of weather conditions. In the last few decades, the transportation of goods across the Bernina Pass has become very important both for the profitability of the railway and the economy of the canton. Today, not only are the tourist trains regularly running the route but so are numerous goods trains carrying fuel oils, petrol, fodder, grain and other goods. Glorious scenery can be enjoyed on this journey in any season. The passenger carriages of the Bernina Express, many with their panoramic roofs, facilitate the viewing of the mountain peaks and the glaciers. The Mörteratsch glacier, for example, is a magnificent sight as the train negotiates the Montebello curve. Sadly, the glacier, like others in the region, is receding. It is a disappointing to report that it was not that many years ago that one could descend from the train at the curve and walk about 100 metres to edge of the glacier - it is now hike of more than 3 km! The Bernina Express departs from one of three stations – Chur, Davos or St Moritz. The total distance from St Moritz to Tirano is 61 km and the longest journey, from Davos or Chur, can take up to 4½ hours. The Trenino Rosso, is the Italian name for the same service from Tirano. For more information visit www.rhb.ch/index.php?id=33?&L=4

The Bernina Express climbing the Bernina Pass between Bernina Diavolezza and Bernina Lagalb towards the Lago Bianca with Munt Pers (3,207 m) in the background. Photograph taken on 6th October, 2006.                *Author*

## CH32 – Ferrovia Monte Generoso

The Monte Generoso is a mountain of an altitude of 1,710 m in the canton of Ticino and located about 15 km south of Lugano. From the summit, the traveller can enjoy a 360º panoramic view of the Italian lakes of Lugano, Como and Maggiore. But that is not all, the vista embraces the city of Lugano, the Po Valley to Milan, the ranges extending from the Gran Paradiso to Monte Rosa, from the Matterhorn to the Jungfrau Massif and from the Gotthard to the Bernina. Since 1890, a railway has been operating here to reach the summit. Trains run every day between April and November and for a month over Christmas and New Year. Services run from Capolago terminus alongside the SBB main line station and travel the 9 km route taking about 36 minutes to reach the summit station at Vetta (alt. 1,592 m). The trains are electrically powered (850V DC) and, because of the gradients, as much as 22 per cent, the rack/cogwheel system designed by Roman Abt is employed. The train includes a covered trailer in which passengers can carry cycles and other personal luggage; many choose to cycle down from the summit. On seven occasions during the year, it is possible to experience a fascinating trip in 'belle époque' style. On these special excursions, an 1890-built (SLM Winterthur) steam locomotive, the oldest one still in operation in Switzerland, is deployed to push the open-sided carriages of about the same vintage to the top; the journey takes 90 minutes. The trains can also be chartered for special events. For more information, the railway has an excellent website published in Italian, German, French and English – see www.montegeneroso.ch The photo gallery on the site is superb giving the potential visitor a taste of things to come.

On 1st October, 2006 a Ferrovia Monte Generoso train leaves the Capolago terminus for the summit. *Author*

## CH33 – Centovalli

This railway, named the Centovalli meaning the 'Valley of the 100 Valleys', perhaps gives the would-be traveller some idea of the terrain through which the route travels. The metre gauge railway is a shared operation between the Swiss operator - Ferrovie Autolinee Regionali Ticinesi - and the Italian counterpart - Società Subalpina di Imprese Ferroviarie. The railway runs 13 km from Locarno to the Swiss/Italian border near Ribellasca and then continues a further 35 km to Domodossola in Italy's Piedmont. This railway is also described in the chapter on Italy (*see entry 19*). The history of this goes back to 1898. From very early on, local politicians on both sides of the frontier had agreed plans to create a railway connecting the two towns. However, it took almost a quarter of a century before this goal was achieved. The companies involved were troubled a number of times with financial problems and the onset of World War I did not help. The Italian side of the operation almost went bankrupt several times and it was necessary for the Swiss to intervene with financial help. Financial problems, incidentally, have continued to dog the railway until quite recently but these have been largely relieved with a new law, enacted in Italy. This legislation allows for better national government support for the country's smaller railway lines including the Centovalli. It has not just been financial difficulties that this railway has had to face. In August 1978, the greatest disaster in the history of the railway was caused by a violent storm when, in just one night, the Italian part of the line was destroyed. Four bridges had to be completely re-built and significant lengths of track re-laid in order to restore services. Although the necessary financial support was immediately forthcoming, it still took more then two years to re-build the line before normal operations could resume. There is much to see on this railway including outstanding steel viaducts crossing the tributaries of the River Melazza. There are seven bridges and 22 tunnels in Switzerland. The impressive steel viaduct near the village of Intragna is awe-inspiring. If one is lucky, one may see the intrepid bungee jumping off the viaduct or even perhaps participate? Very recently, new 'panoramic' carriages have been introduced which allow for the better viewing of this fantastic scenery. More information can be found at www.centovalli.ch

# Appendix

## Rack/Cogwheel Systems

The Alpine Railways, because of the mountainous nature of the terrain, often require an additional system of propulsion which will allow trains, that could not rely on normal adhesion alone, to negotiate steep gradients. This requirement led to the invention of the various rack/cogwheel systems which have played a crucial part in bringing railways to otherwise inaccessible locations.

There are four perhaps five main types of rack/cogwheel systems. The Riggenbach system was invented by Niklaus Riggenbach and is the oldest form of rack railway/cogwheel system. It is formed by steel plates or channels connected by round or square rods at regular intervals. The Riggenbach system was the first devised but suffers from the fact that its fixed rack is much more complex and expensive to build than the other, later designs. Incidentally, this system is sometimes also referred to as the Marsh system, because of simultaneous invention by an American inventor of that name who was the builder of the Mount Washington Cog Railway in the United States of America.

The rack/cogwheel system designed by Roman Abt is the one in most popular in use in the Alps. Here on Austria's Schafbergbahn one can clearly see the teeth of the parallel plates which make up the rack. Photo taken on 30th June, 2007. *Author*

The Abt system was devised by Roman Abt, a Swiss locomotive engineer. Abt at this time was working for a rack/cogwheel railway which used the Riggenbach design which he thought could be improved. The Abt rack features steel plates mounted vertically and in parallel to the rails, with rack teeth machined to a precise profile within them. These engage with the locomotive's pinion teeth much more smoothly than the Riggenbach system. Two or three parallel sets of Abt rack plates are used, with a corresponding number of driving pinions on the locomotive, to ensure that at least one pinion tooth is always engaged securely. Today, the majority of rack/cogwheel railways in the Alps use the Abt system. Incidentally, it is sometimes referred to as the double lamella system.

The Strub system was invented by Emil Strub and is similar to the Abt system but uses just one wide rack plate welded on top of a flat bottomed 'T' shaped rail. It is the simplest rack system to maintain and as a consequence has become increasingly popular in use.

The Locher system was invented by Eduard Locher and involves teeth cut in the sides rather than the top of the rail. It is engaged on each side of the rail by two cogwheels on the locomotive. The system allows steeper gradients to be negotiated than the other systems, whose teeth could otherwise 'jump' out of the rack. It is used in only one location in Switzerland, the Pilatus Railway (*see entry CH24*) which at 48 per cent has the steepest gradient of any rack railway in the world.

A fifth system is one devised by the Von Roll company, a Swiss aerial tramway and industrial manufacturing company. It was later taken over by the Austrian manufacturer Doppelmayr in 1996. The system is similar to that of Roman Abt's except that the teeth in the single blade are cut to suit the gear design either of the Riggenbach or the Strub cogwheels. Because of its simplicity, the Von Roll rack replaces Riggenbach or Strub racks in new or renewed installations, thus avoiding the greater expense of replacing the cogs on existing steam-driven or electric-powered locomotives and railcars.

However, railways operating on steep gradients are obliged to operate by rack/cogwheel only. This means that the locomotive's wheels freewheel and, despite appearances to the contrary, do not contribute in any way to the propulsion of the train.

Some railway systems are referred to as 'rack-and-adhesion' because they use the cog drive only on the steepest sections where normal adhesion would fail. Elsewhere on the route they operate like any other adhesion only type traction.

Originally, almost all of the rack/cogwheel railways were powered by steam-driven locomotives. These had to be extensively modified to work effectively. Unlike a diesel- or electric-powered locomotive, the steam locomotive only works when its source of power - the boiler - is level or fairly close to it. A locomotive's boiler requires water to cover the boiler tubes and firebox at all times which, if it does not, will give way under pressure causing failure, sometimes catastrophic. In order that such steam locomotives succeed, the boiler, cab and general superstructure of the locomotive have to be tilted forward so that when climbing the gradient they become horizontal.

As a consequence, locomotives of this design, for opposing reasons, cannot function on level track. It is necessary, therefore, that the entire line, including inside the maintenance sheds, is kept on a gradient. These difficulties with steam traction, particularly the cost of building and running such locomotives, was one of the main reasons why rack/cogwheel railways were among the first to be electrified. Most of today's rack railways operate on an electricity supply but not all, for example, the Brienz-Rothorn Bahn (*see entry CH21*). The observer will also notice that rack/cogwheel locomotives, for safety reasons, always push their passenger carriages up gradients and lead them down. The reason for this being that the locomotives are fitted with powerful brakes, often including hooks or clamps which can give maximum grip to the rack rail. Some locomotives are also fitted with automatic brakes that are applied should the set maximum speed be exceeded. Often there is no coupler between the locomotive and first carriage of the train as gravity will always rule the day. The maximum speed of trains operating on a rack/cogwheel railway rarely exceeds 25 kmh.

# Glossary

| German | French | Italian | English |
|---|---|---|---|
| autowagen | train auto | carico d'automobli | vehicle carrier |
| bahn | reseau | ferrovia | railway |
| bahnunternehmen | enterprise ferroviaire | ferovia impresa | railway company |
| bahnhof, station | gare | stazione | station |
| betriebslänge | longueur exploitée | lunghazza escercita | route length |
| doppelstockwagen | voiture à deux niveaux | carrozza a due piani | double-deck coach |
| eigentumslänge | longeur du proper réseau | lunghezza della propria rete | length of line owned |
| Eurospaische bahnen | réseaux européens | ferrovie europee | European railways |
| fahrplan | horaire | orario | timetable |
| fahrzeuge | véhicules | veicoli | rolling stock |
| fahrleitung | ligne de contact | linea di contatto | catenary |
| gleis | voie/quai | binario | track/platform |
| gepäckwagen | fourgons | bagaglia | baggage car |
| güterwagen | wagons | carri merci | goods wagon |
| güterzug | train merchandises | treno merci | freight train |
| lokomotiven | locomotives | veicoli motori | locomotives |
| neigezug | train pendulaire | treno ad asserto variabile | tilting train |
| normalspur | voie normal | a scartamento normale | standard gauge |
| niveauubergang | passage à niveau | passaggio a livello | level crossing |
| personenwagen | voiture | carroze viaggiatori | passenger carriage |
| personenverkehr | voyageurs | traffico viaggiatori | passenger traffic |
| rangierfahrzeuge | locotracteurs | veicoli motori di manovra | shunters |
| reisezug | train voyageur | treno viaggiatori | passenger train |
| rollmaterial | matériel roulant | materiale rotabile | rolling stock |
| schmalspur | voie étroite | a scartamento ridotto | narrow gauge |
| steuerwagen | voitures de commande | veicoli di comando | railcar (unpowered) |
| trasse | sillon | traccia d'orario | train path |
| triebwagen | autorail | automotrici | railcar (powered) |
| unfälle | accidents | infortuni | accidents |
| unterhalt | entretien | manutenzione | maintenance |
| weiche | aiguillage | scambio | points |
| zug | train | treno | train |

| Slovenian | Croatian | English |
|---|---|---|
| *prihod* | *dolazak* | arrivals |
| *odhod* | *odlazak* | departures |
| *prvorazreden* | *fprvu klasu* | first class |
| *drugorezreden* | *drugu klasu* | second class |
| *kolodvor* | *stanica* | railway station |
| *platforma* | *platforma* | platform |
| *enosmerna (vozoovnica)* | *kartu u jednom pravcu* | single |
| *povratna* | *povratnu kartu* | return |
| *Spalnik* | *spavaca kola* | sleeper (car) |
| *vstopnica/karta* | *kartu* | ticket |
| *vlak* | *vlak* | train |

# Abbreviations

| | |
|---|---|
| CFF | Chemins de fer Fédéraux Suisses |
| DB | Deutsche Bahn |
| FFS | Ferrovie federali svizzere |
| FS | Ferrovie dello Stato. Trenitalia is the primary operator of trains within Italy. Trenitalia is owned by Ferrovie dello Stato, itself owned by the Italian Government. |
| GTT | Gruppo Torinese Trasporti SpA |
| ÖBB | Österreichische Bundesbahnen |
| PLM | Compagnie des Chemins de Fer de Paris à Lyon et à la Méditerranée |
| RFF | Reseau Ferré de France |
| RFI | Rete Ferroviaria Italiana |
| SBB | Schweizerische Bundesbahnen |
| SNCF | Société Nationale des Chemins de fer Français |
| TER | Transport Express Régional |
| TGV | Train Grande Vitesse (high speed train) |

# Bibliography

(All publications are in the English language unless indicated otherwise)

*Books and Journals*

*Austrian Railways - Locomotives, Multiple Units and Trams - European Handbook No. 3* by Brian Garvin and Peter Fox. Platform 5 Publishing, Sheffield 2005. ISBN 1-902336-49-6

*Italian Railways - European Handbook No. 6* by David Haydock. Platform 5 Publishing, Sheffield 2007. ISBN 1-902336-56-9

*French Railways – European Handbook No. 4* by David Haydock. Platform 5 Publishing, Sheffield 2008. ISBN 978 1-902336-65-7

*Great Railway Journeys of Europe* edited by Tom Le Bas of Insight Guides, London 2005. ISBN 981-234-720-8

*The Encyclopaedia of Trains and Locomotives*, edited by Davis Ross, Amber Books, London 2003. ISBN 1-85605-792-5

*Austria. Insight Guides*, London 2006. ISBN 13-078 981 258 342 0

*Germany – Eyewitness Travel Guides* published by Dorling Kindersley Ltd, London 2007. ISBN 1-4053-1218-1

*Die Mariazellerbahn* by Horst Felsinger and Walter Schober, 3rd edition, Verlag Pospischil, Vienna (de)

*Die Erzbergbahnen* by Mike Morton *et al.* Austria Railway Group, Carlisle 2005

*The Mur Valley - Unzmarkt-Tamsweg-Mautendorf and die Murtalbahn* by Stephen R. Ford. The Austrian Railway Group, Carlisle 2005

*Die Eisenbahn in Österreich - Geschichte, Strecken, Lokomotiven* by Klaus J. Vetter, Geramond 2007. ISBN 978-3-7654-7092-9

*Österreich mit dem Zug erlebeb* by Inderst, Gohl and Schönborn, Geramond München, 2000. ISBN 3-932785-72- X

*Die Alpen mit dem Zug entdecken* by Marcus Inderst. Geramond München, 2006. ISBN 3-7654-7187-9

*Die Schonsten Alpenbahnen - Strecken - Zuge - Landschaften* by Dietmar Beckman and Bernd Eisenschink. GeraNova Bruckmann München, 2004. ISBN 3 86517 031 5

*History of the Austrian Railway* by Alfred Horn and published by ÖBB on the internet (see website entries)

*100 Jahre Strassenbahnen in Innsbruck 1891-1991 + 50 Jahre Innsbrucker Verkehrsbetriebe AG 1941-1991* Tiroler Museumsbahnen, Innsbruck 1991.

*75 Jahre Mittenwaldbahn* ÖBB undated

*Bahn-Jahrbuch Schweiz 2006* edited by Peter Hürzeler and Hans-Bernard Schönborn, Edition Lan AG, Zug 2006. ISBN 3-906691-28-4 (de)

*Bernina Express Travel Guide* by Photoglob AG 2001. ISBN 3-907594-01-0

*Die SBB Brunigbahn*, by Bear Moser and Thomas Küstner, Eisenbahn Journal, Fürstenfeldbruch 1996. ISBN 3-922404-85-5 (de)

*Die Rhätische Bahn macht Dampf* by Christian Müller, Foto Geiger Flims, Davos 1998. ISBN 3-9520828-5-6 (de)

*Glacier Express - from St Moritz to Zermatt* by Klaus Eckert and Ilona Eckert, Travel House Media (Merian Live!) Munich 2005. ISBN 3-8342-9505-1

*Great Railway Journeys of Europe* edited by Tom Le Bas of Insight Guides, London 2005. ISBN 981-234-720-8

*Les Chemins de Fer Rhetiques*, published by Eisenbahn Journal, Fürstenfeldbruch undated. ISSN 0986-6663

*Mountain Rack Railways of Switzerland* by J.R. Bardsley, Oakwood Press, Usk 1999. ISBN 0-85361-511-X

*Switzerland – Eyewitness Travel Guides*, by Adriana Czupryn, Malgorzata Omilanowska and Ulrich Schwendimann, Dorling Kindersley, London 2005. ISBN 13—978-4055-0292-0 & 10-1-4053-2092-5

*Swiss Museum of Transport – Highlights Guide* published by Verkehrshaus der Schweiz, Luzern 2006

*The Complete Encyclopaedia of Locomotives* by Mirco de Cet And Alan Kent. Rebo International, The Netherlands 2006. ISBN 13-978-90-366-1505-1 & 10-90-366-1504-4

*The Essential Guide to French Heritage and Tourist Railways* by Mervyn Jones, Oakwood Press, Usk 2006. ISBN 0-85361-648-1

*The Essential Guide to Swiss Heritage and Tourist Railways* by Mervyn Jones, Oakwood Press, Usk 2007. ISBN 978 0-85361-659 7

*The Essential Guide to Austrian Railways and Tramways* by Mervyn Jones, Oakwood Press, Usk 2008. ISBN 978 0-85361-674-0

*The Swiss Railway Saga – 150 Years of Swiss Trains* by Hans Peter Treichler *et al.* AS Verlag & Buchkonzept, Zurich 1996. ISBN 3-905111-16-0

*Trains Alpines* - marketing brochure published by Schweiz Tourismus (MySwitzerland.com) 2006

*Trains du massif du Mont-Blanc* by Beat Moser, Le Train-Editions Publitrains eurl, Betshdorf 2000. ISSN 1267-5008

*Musée français du Chemin de Fer Mulhouse – Histoire, Projets, Collection* – Numéro spécial 24 ans du Musée No 438-96/3. Editions AFAC, 1996 Paris. ISSN 1252 – 9907

*Musée français du Chemin de Fer Mulhouse* by M. Jean Renaud et autres. Mulhouse Musée, 1989. ISBN 2-9501041-0-X

*Connaissance des Arts – Cité du Train* edited by Guy Boyer. SPFA, 2005 Paris. (ISSN 1242 – 9198)

*Cité du Train – Le Catalogue* edited by Philippe Mirville. Editions La Vie du Rail, 2005. ISBN 2-915 034-34-6

*The Story of the Train, Board and Trustees of the Science Museum* (National Rail Museum), GB-London 1999. (ISBN 1 872826) (English language)

*Le Chemin de Fer de la Mure*. SOFITEC, undated Paris.

*The History of Trains* by Colin Garratt. Chancellor Press, 1998 London. ISBN 0 7537 0630 X (English)

Journals of the UK-based SNCF Society - from edition number 113 to present day (Spring 2009)

Journals of the UK-based Austrian Railway Group - from edition number 60 to present day (Spring 2009)

*Swiss Express* (UK-based Swiss Railways Society magazine) - from March 2003 edition to present day (March 2009)

*Independent Travellers Europe by Rail*, edited by Tim Locke published by Thomas Cook Publishing, Peterborough UK 2006. ISBN1 841574 95 3

*Les trains des Alpes* by Jean Tricoire. Le Train Special No 57 - Editions Publitrain eurl, BP 10, F-67660 Betschdorf 2009. ISSN 1267 - 5008

### Maps

*Eisenbahnatlas Österreich* (Rail Atlas Austria). Schweers + Wall, Köln 2005. ISBN 3-89494-128-6

*Eisenbahnatlas Schweiz* (Rail Atlas Switzerland). Schweers + Wall, Köln 2004. ISBN 3-89494-122-7

*Eisenbahnatlas Deutschland* (Rail Atlas Germany). Schweers + Wall, Köln 2007. ISBN 3-89494-136-9

*Rail Map - Europe*, 16th Edition published by Thomas Cook Publishing. ISBN 978-1-84157-677-0

*European Railway Atlas - Italy* privately produced and published by M.G. Ball 2007

*European Railway Atlas - France* privately produced and published by M.G. Ball 2007-8

*Michelin Maps* for France (south), Italy, Austria, Germany and Switzerland published by Michelin Travel Publications, Watford UK, 2006-8.

*La France Vue du Rail* – Cartes des Chemins de Fer Touristiques. UNECTO, 2007

### Railway Magazines

*Today's Railways – Europe*. Published by Platform 5 Publishing Ltd, Sheffield, UK and produced monthly in English.

*Le Train* - Editions Publitrain eurl, BP 10, F-67660 Betschdorf (monthly in French).

# Websites

www.oebb.at/en the official ÖBB website providing a wealth of information as well as timetable and fares information.

www.rail-guides.eu – website written by the author to support this book and others (en).

www.steane.com/egtre/egtre.htm - a useful website about European Railways maintained by Paul Steane.

www.railfaneurope.net

www.nostalgiebahn.at/

www.erlebnisbahn.at

reiseauskunft.bahn.de/bin/query.exe/en the on-line timetable for most European services.

www.austria.info/english/ the official site for Austrian Tourist Information.

www.oebb.at/en/OeBB_Group/History_of_the_Austrian_Railway/index.jsp – history of Austrian railways.

www.srpc.ch – photographic catalogue of Swiss railway companies operating on narrow and standard gauge tracks  (de).

www.photos-trains.ch – another interesting photographic album (de fr).

www.seak.ch - a long standing Zurich Club (formed 1933) which publishes the *Eisenbahn Amateur* - see also their website www.eisenbahn-amateur.ch (de fr en nl).

www.railclub.ch  - website of the Rail club of Montreux (fr).

www.lok-remise.ch - website of 'Kreissegment-Lokomotiv-Remise der Schweiz' - an organization focused on railway architecture including locomotive sheds and roundhouses (de).

www.dampfschleuder.ch - website dedicated to the Xrotd R 12 snow blower (de).

www.ag2.ch - website for enthusiastic supporters of Appenzellbahnen (de).

www.trittbrett.ch - website dedicated to Bern transport of yesteryear (de).

www.rheinschauen.ch - website for a museum at Lustenau on the Austrian side of the Rhine 2 km from the Swiss town of Au which portrays some items of railway history (de).

www.sbb.ch – website of the Swiss Federal Railways (de fr it en).

www.swisstravelsystem.ch – website addressing most travel needs in Switzerland (de fr it en).

www.swiss-rail.ch – another website written by rail enthusiasts (de).

www.rail-info.ch/index.en.html - a very useful website written by Stefan Dringenberg, Klaus P. Canavan and Manfred Luckmann and which was particularly helpful to the author in his early research (de en).

www.myswitzerland.com/de/loco/lok.cfm - a webcam mounted on a train with continously changing views of the tracks, stations, and landscape. This site also links to another useful source of images and information - www.ferrosteph.net/ferrosteph/sbb/ (fr en ).

www.swissworld.org/eng - a very useful website but all aspects of Swiss life. To learn more about Swiss Railways and save time finding the link the following URL will help - www.swissworld.org/eng/swissworld.html?siteSect=907&sid=5385230&rubricId=17145 (en).

www.x-rail.ch – another superb photographic gallery with a wealth of useful information (de).

www.stadlerrail.com - website of the Swiss engineering company, successor to SLM at Winterthur and other companies (de en).

www.wikipedia.org - the free encyclopedia and http://commons.wikimedia.org  both sites have proven to be very useful during the research but given the freedom that the general public have to contribute/edit material it is always important to verify content.

www.oakwoodpress.co.uk – publisher's website listing their UK and European titles (en).

# Addresses

**The SNCF Society,** c/o 5 Middle Furlong, Seaford, Sussex, BN25 1SR

**The Italian Railway Society**, c/o 1A Clyde Road, Wood Green, London, N22 7AD

**Austrian Railways Group,** c/o Howard Lawrence, 14 Wheatfield Way, Skegby, NG17 3EU

**The German Railway Society**, c/o Tony Wright, Sutton, Hendra Barton, Truro, Cornwall, TR1 3TL

**Swiss Railways Society**, c/o Membership Secretary, 28 Appletree Lane, Redditch, Worcestershire B97 6SE. E-mail: membership@SwissRailSoc.org.uk

**Rail Europe** is located at the French Travel Centre, 178 Piccadilly, London W1. Telephone: 08708 371371 Website: www.raileurope.co.uk  E-mail: reservations@raileurope.co.uk

**The Railway Touring Company**, 14A Tuesday Market Place, King's Lynn PE30 1JN.  Telephone: 01553 661500 Fax: 01553 661800. Website: www.railwaytouring.co.uk e-mail: enquiries@railwaytouring.co.uk British company which frequently runs excursions in Europe, France (and elsewhere) often using heritage locomotives.

**Railtrail Tours Ltd**, 43 St Edward Street, Leek, ST13 5DN
Telephone: 01538 38 23 23 Fax: 01538 38 25 25 Website: www.railtrail.co.uk E-mail: enquiry@railtrail.co.uk Another British company which runs excursions to France and elsewhere.

**Travelsphere Ltd**, Compass House, Rockingham Road, Market Harborough, Leicestershire LE16 7QD Telephone: 0870 240 2426. Website: www.travelsphere.co.uk/website/intros/rail-intro.aspx

**Venice-Simplon Express Ltd.**, Sea Containers House, 20 Upper Ground, London SE1 9PF. Telephone: 020 7805 5060 www.orient-express.com

**The Oakwood Press**, PO Box 13, Usk, Mon., NP15 1YS.  Website: www.oakwoodpress.co.uk  E-mail: sales@oakwoodpress.co.uk

# Index